# PLESSY
## v.
# FERGUSON

Separate but Equal

# GREAT SUPREME COURT DECISIONS

Brown v. Board of Education
Dred Scott v. Sandford
Engel v. Vitale
Marbury v. Madison
Miranda v. Arizona
Plessy v. Ferguson
Regents of the University of California v. Bakke
Roe v. Wade

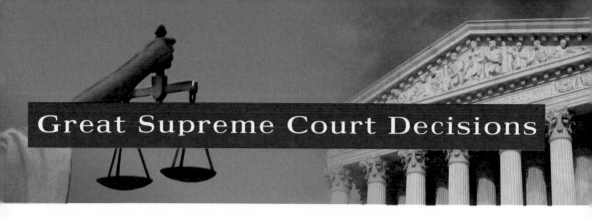

# Great Supreme Court Decisions

# PLESSY
# v.
# FERGUSON

Separate but Equal

# Tim McNeese

## CHELSEA HOUSE
### PUBLISHERS
An imprint of Infobase Publishing

**Plessy v. Ferguson**

Chelsea House
An imprint of Infobase Publishing
132 West 31st Street
New York NY 10001

**Library of Congress Cataloging-in-Publication Data**
McNeese, Tim.
  Plessy v. Ferguson : separate but equal/ Tim McNeese.
      p. cm.—(Great Supreme Court decisions)
  Includes bibliographical references and index.
  ISBN 0-7910-9237-2 (hardcover)
    1.   Plessy, Homer Adolph—Trials, litigation, etc.—Juvenile literature.
2. Segregation in transportation—Law and legislation—Louisiana—History—
Juvenile literature. 3. Segregation—Law and legislation—United States—His-
tory—Juvenile literature. 4. United States—Race relations—History—Juvenile
literature. I. Title. II. Title: Plessy versus Ferguson. III. Series.
      KF223.P56M36 2006
      342.7308'73—dc22                                           2006007325

Series design by Erika K. Arroyo
Cover design by Takeshi Takahashi

Printed in the United States of America

Bang EJB 10 9 8 7 6 5 4 3 2 1

This book is printed on acid-free paper.

All links and Web addresses were checked and verified to be correct at the time of publication. Because of the dynamic nature of the Web, some addresses and links may have changed since publication and may no longer be valid.

# Contents

# Introduction

The weather was typical for a summer day in New Orleans, also known as the Crescent City. The temperature hovered at a muggy 86 degrees and all across the city, the sky was cloudy. It could have been any other day in the cosmopolitan world of New Orleans. At the city's Press Street Depot, people stood on the platform waiting for the arrival of a train belonging to the East Louisiana Railroad. The Press Street Depot was a hustling, bustling stop on the line, its station flanking crowded railroad yards just off of the local street known as Faubourg Marigny. The station actually served two railroads, the East Louisiana Railroad and the New Orleans and Northeastern Railroad. Outside, additional railroad facilities, including a coal yard and freight sheds, bordered the depot. The depot itself was a complex of railroad offices and train sheds. There was even a restaurant. The broad waters of the Mississippi River flowed near the station. All along the depot's boarding platform and near the ticket office window, posters announced a newly passed state law: the Separate Car Act.

Scattered across the station's wooden platform, would-be passengers held their tickets for the railroad's Queen and Crescent Line. The line ran north from the station through a heavily wooded swamp and on toward the northern reaches of Louisiana. The Number Eight Train would cross a seven-mile bridge across Lake Pontchartrain and then make scheduled stops at a string of small Louisiana towns, including Lewisburg, Mandeville, and Abita Springs. This line was new for the East Louisiana Railroad, the tracks having just been laid earlier that year. On the platform, nothing seemed unusual—just another day of passengers buying tickets, readying to ride the rails, Southern men and women headed north across eastern Louisiana.

On this cloudy Tuesday afternoon, the train was scheduled to roll into the station, take on its usual complement of passengers and then, with the conductor's permission, roll out again at 4:15 bound for the town of Covington, located on the opposite side of Lake Pontchartrain. Covington was the end of the line, the destination of tourists. Advertisements printed by the East Louisiana Railroad touted Covington as "the healthiest spot in America."[1] The train would move along slowly, taking two hours to cover the 30 miles from New Orleans to Covington. Its pace would match that of New Orleans itself—slow and easy, with no one in a hurry and no one going far. It was just another train bound north out of New Orleans on a summer day. The train wouldn't even leave the state of Louisiana: Its tracks only ran within the state's borders.

## PLESSY BUYS A TICKET

On this day, June 7, 1892, one of the would-be passengers was a young Louisiana native, a man in his late 20s who was rehearsing for the pages of history. The young man was preparing to board a train for reasons quite different from everyone else.

He had specific instructions, and he was basically following a script. The instructions he had been given were simple, almost mundane: He was to buy a ticket at the depot and board the first-class carriage of the Queen and Crescent Line of the East Louisiana Railroad. This passenger's plan had third and fourth steps, however. Once he boarded the train's first-class car, the man was to get himself arrested and taken to jail, where he was to be booked for the crime of being black and attempting to ride in a whites-only railcar.

As he stood on the depot platform, however, Homer Plessy did not appear any different from the other men and women waiting for the train. After all, 20,000 people rode on the East Louisiana Railroad every year. Despite his appearance, however, Plessy's purpose for being there that day, ticket in hand, was extremely different from that of his fellow passengers. They had bought tickets as commuters, workers who rode every day from their homes outside New Orleans to their jobs in the big city. Others rode this train, buying excursion tickets for one dollar to ride across the lake to enjoy the beaches along Lake Pontchartrain. Plessy had a greater purpose that day. He wasn't a commuter or a tourist. He was there to test a Louisiana law and its constitutionality.

The law was Louisiana's Separate Car Act, one of the many laws that had been passed by a white-dominated Louisiana state legislature. The law was simple, straightforward, and prejudicial:

> All railway companies carrying passengers in their coaches in this state shall provide equal but separate accommodations for the white, and colored races, by providing two or more passenger coaches for each train. No person or persons shall be permitted to occupy seats in coaches, other than the ones assigned to them, on account of the race they belong to.[2]

The statute required railroad officials, including train conductors, to enforce the law. Those who did not were subject to punishment: Anyone caught violating the law was subject to a

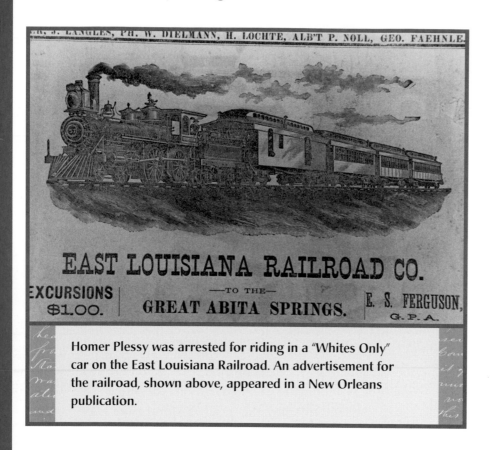

EAST LOUISIANA RAILROAD CO.

EXCURSIONS $1.00.     —TO THE—    GREAT ABITA SPRINGS.    E. S. FERGUSON, G. P. A.

Homer Plessy was arrested for riding in a "Whites Only" car on the East Louisiana Railroad. An advertisement for the railroad, shown above, appeared in a New Orleans publication.

$25 fine or 20 days in jail. Homer Plessy knew the risks he was taking that day.

Such statutes were known as "Jim Crow" laws, and they were designed to discriminate and treat blacks as inferiors. Such laws were not new in 1892. They had been on the books in various states for more than half a century. Ironically, the first such "separate car law" was passed in 1841 in a Northern state, Massachusetts. Before the Civil War, Massachusetts had been one of the most important antislavery states.

## THE CONFRONTATION

As Homer Plessy readied to board the train that afternoon, he drew no attention. He was just another white passenger, a well-dressed man wearing a business suit and hat. He might have passed for a gentleman of means—he was, after all, traveling first class. Homer Plessy was not what he seemed to be, however. He was a Trojan horse. This young gentleman appeared white, but, because the equivalent of one of his eight great-grandparents had been black, he was considered black by Louisiana law.

As Homer Plessy readied himself to defy Louisiana law and board the first-class car, he took his place in the line of ticket holders. He walked past the train's additional cars, including those marked "colored only." When the conductor finally called for the passengers to board the Number Eight Train, Plessy stepped onto the first-class car's platform and entered a world officially forbidden to him. The car was elegant and grand. The interior was rich with mahogany, and rows of brass lamps lined both sides of the car. The passengers' seats were plush, designed for comfort, and adjustable. The car was clean, even pristine. At both ends of the car were toilet rooms, each fitted with grand fixtures and tiled mirrors. For Plessy, who made his living as a shoemaker, it was the finest railroad car he had ever stepped foot in. It was not his first time to board a first-class car, however. Plessy was so light skinned that, although officially defined as a black man, he could easily pass for white. He had done so before. More than once, he had bought first-class tickets and had been a passenger on a whites-only rail car. He had done so without drawing attention. As he boarded this train, no one questioned him. Quietly, he took a seat in the car designed for those of another race.

Outside, the time for departure approaching, the engineer blew the train's whistle and the conductor closed the doors on the cars. A sharp blast of steam shot into the air from the train's engine, and the passengers felt the train begin to move forward slowly, its great iron wheels squealing. The passengers in the first-class car began to search for their tickets. The conductor, J. J. Dowling, walked down the aisle in his usual fashion, collecting those tickets. Everything appeared as it should have been, according to Louisiana law. The first-class car carried white passengers, and the colored-only car carried black passengers—all except for Homer Plessy.

Then, just as the train was beginning to move forward, so did a series of planned events. When Conductor Dowling reached Plessy's seat, the railroad official asked for his ticket. Only then did the unassuming Louisiana shoemaker explain what soon became a concern for his fellow passengers: "I have to tell you," Plessy said to Dowling, "that according to Louisiana law, I am a colored man."[3]

By admitting he was black, Homer Plessy set in motion a chain of events that would unfold over the next four years. What began as a minor infraction of Louisiana law would end as a cause célèbre, an explosive case that would land on the docket of the United States Supreme Court. Even as late as the last decade of the nineteenth century, the United States was a nation divided by race and prejudice. Laws filled the statute books, hundreds, even thousands, of them, all designed to keep the black race in a constant state of second-class citizenship. Despite the bloody civil war that had ended slavery, and national policy that had tried, for 12 years to elevate former slaves to a status equal to any white man, that equality had not come. Many state laws had been created to not only deny rights to America's blacks, but to strip them of the rights they had gained only a generation earlier.

EQUAL·JUSTICE·UNDER·LAW·

# 1

# Promises
# Not Kept

T he nineteenth century delivered extraordinary change to
America's 4 million slaves. Slavery had existed in America
since the mid-seventeenth century, more than a century before
the 13 British colonies won independence from Great Britain
through the Revolutionary War. That conflict had resulted in
a significant decline in slavery in the northern states. Slavery
continued in the southern states, however, even as Americans
adopted a way of life independent of British tyranny.

In the newly formed United States of the 1780s, slavery was
indeed in transition—but it was far from dead. America's Found-
ing Fathers—Thomas Jefferson, John Adams, Patrick Henry,
and others—may have agreed to the words of the *Declaration*

The invention of the cotton gin increased the production of cotton and prolonged the institution of slavery.

*of Independence* that read "all Men are created equal, that they are endowed by their Creator with certain unalienable Rights" in 1776, but slavery existed even after all of the men who had established the new United States were dead and gone.

## SLAVERY AND WAR

Falling tobacco prices in the last decades of the 1700s appeared to many to signal a final collapse of slavery in North America, but the institution received a shot in the arm in the early 1790s. In 1793, Eli Whitney invented the cotton gin, a simple device that separated seeds from cotton fiber, helping to make cotton production profitable. With that single stroke of mechanical genius, slavery was destined to continue for another three generations. When its end came, it did so through the events that encompassed America's fiercest trial, the Civil War (1861–1865). Driven by sectional rivalries and the necessity to protect the future of slavery, 11 Southern slave-holding states seceded from the Union between December 1860 and June 1861. One of the primary goals of the Civil War was to decide the question of whether the United States would remain one country or become two; a secondary goal for the North, under the leadership of President Abraham Lincoln, became the ultimate destruction of slavery. During that monumental American struggle, more than 620,000 men died. When the smoke cleared, slavery was also dead and the Union was restored.

At the end of the Civil War, the future of America's black population had never appeared brighter. President Lincoln had issued his Emancipation Proclamation, which had gone into effect on January 1, 1863, a first step in freeing millions of slaves. The Northern-led United States Congress had passed the Thirteenth Amendment to the U.S. Constitution, completely

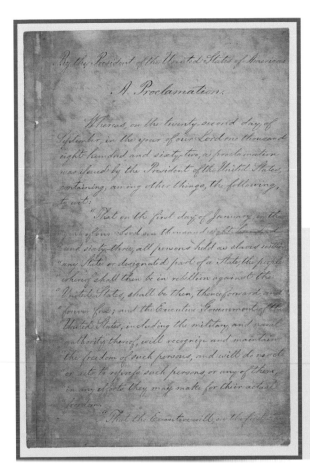

On January 1, 1863, President Abraham Lincoln issued the Emancipation Proclamation, declaring that all slaves in the rebelling states of the Confederacy "henceforward shall be free."

abolishing slavery, during the final months of the war in the early spring of 1865. (The amendment was ratified by the states in December 1865.) The following year, Congress passed the Fourteenth Amendment (ratified in 1868), which guaranteed citizenship for all former slaves. Just 11 years earlier, in 1857, the U.S. Supreme Court had decided that all blacks in America were "a subordinate and inferior class of beings" and that they "had no rights that white people were bound to respect."[4] In 1870, the Fifteenth Amendment was added to the Constitution by Congress and promised the vote to black men. As the amendment was worded, "The right of citizens of the United States to vote shall not be denied or abridged by the United States or by any State on account of race, color, or previous condition of servitude."[5] For those who had campaigned for decades, including abolitionists both black and white, the amendment represented "the culmination of the crusade to end slavery and give black people the same rights as white people."[6]

## FREEDMEN AND BLACK CODES

At first, white Southerners attempted to limit the political and social successes of the newly freed black populations. In 1865 and 1866, white leaders across the South met in their respective state capitals to determine the future of former slaves. White-dominated Southern legislatures passed laws that became known as Black Codes. These laws were designed to restrict the freedoms of blacks across the South. Former slaves—called "freedmen"—were required to sign labor contracts with white landowners, often tying them to the very lands that they had worked as slaves. Although they varied, the Black Codes typically kept blacks from owning firearms or alcohol, purchasing property, making legal contracts, testifying in court, and serving on juries. These restrictive laws forbade blacks from even entering many storefronts, hotels and inns, public restrooms, and public means of transportation, such as ferries, steamboats, and trains. In some Southern states, blacks were not allowed to attend schools or to learn to read. Above all, perhaps, these new laws denied blacks the right to vote.

These attempts to destroy the new freedoms of blacks across the South were often thwarted by federal laws, such as the Thirteenth, Fourteenth, and Fifteenth Amendments. Radical Northerners in Congress led the way in this effort. In early 1866, a moderate Republican senator from Illinois, Lyman Trumbull, introduced a pair of bills designed to protect Southern blacks. The first was intended to provide monies for the Freedmen's Bureau. This agency—known officially as the Bureau of Refugees, Freedmen, and Abandoned Lands—had been created by Congress in early 1865. Its initial purpose was to provide federal assistance to former slaves in their transition to freedom:

> The bureau . . . was to help freedmen obtain land; gain an education; negotiate labor contracts with white planters; settle legal and criminal disputes involving black and white people; and provide food, medical care, and transportation for black and white people left destitute by the war.[7]

Trumbull intended to extend the Freedmen's Bureau's authority to help protect black men's right to vote. His second proposal was, in effect, "the first civil rights bill in American history."[8] Its intention was clear: It declared that anyone born in the United States (with the exception, ironically, of American Indians) was a citizen and guaranteed his rights. To give the law additional teeth in the face of Southern opposition, the legislation threatened to deny representation in Congress to any state that attempted to block black men from voting.

The bill was opposed by President Andrew Johnson, but Congress overrode his veto and passed the Civil Rights Act of 1866, followed by the Reconstruction Act of 1867, which dismantled the new, postwar white governments of the Southern states and replaced their elected congressmen and representatives. The Reconstruction Act also divided the Confederate South into five military districts, ruling them with near martial law.

These federal efforts in support of blacks took place in the context of an important era in American history. Reconstruction (1865–1877) lasted  three times longer than the war itself. During those crucial years, blacks were allowed to run for both state and national offices. By the early 1870s, hundreds of black men had been elected to the legislatures of every Southern state that had supported the Confederate government during the Civil War. Blacks also were elected to the United States Congress. Across the South, there were 41 black sheriffs and 5 black mayors. In the Southern cities of Tallahassee, Florida, and Little Rock, Arkansas, blacks served as police chiefs. Politically, a new day had dawned for America's Southern black population.

## THE CHALLENGE TO FREEDOM

These changes could not be made without the notice of blacks everywhere. The dark days of slavery were gone, and in their place were opportunities being laid at the feet of America's newly freed race. Perhaps some—both black and white—thought that the future would evolve differently for blacks and all minorities in America. This sort of wishful thinking and hopeful sentiment was embodied in a speech delivered in 1872 by Jonathan J. Wright, a black associate justice of the South Carolina Supreme Court who had worked alongside the great black abolitionist leader Frederick Douglass in the struggle to abolish slavery. Wright expressed his hope for a future America in which race would play no important role in establishing the direction and the leadership of the country that had so recently emerged from its bloodiest war ever, a war fought in part over slavery:

> Let us with a fixed, firm, hearty, earnest, and unswerving determination move steadily on and on, fanning the flame of true liberty until the last vestige of oppression shall be destroyed, and when that eventful period shall arrive, when, in the selection of rulers, both State and Federal, we shall know no North, no East, no South, no

GLIMPSES AT THE FREEDMEN'S BUREAU—ISSUING RATIONS TO THE OLD AND SICK.—FROM A SKETCH BY OUR SPECIAL ARTIST, JAS. E. TAYLOR.

**This woodcut from 1866 shows a group of elderly and ill people receiving rations from the Freedmen's Bureau. The government agency was formed to help freedmen and white refugees of the Civil War.**

West, no white nor colored, no Democrat nor Republican, but shall choose men because of their moral and intrinsic value, their honesty and integrity, their love of unmixed liberty, and their ability to perform well the duties to be committed to their charge.[9]

Despite pressures exerted by the federal government, many white Southerners were not prepared to surrender the single principle that guided their political and social attitudes toward blacks: that blacks were inferior in every way. Their racism was built on the concept that blacks were simply not capable of achieving at the level of whites and, therefore, should be treated as unequal. Theirs was an attitude not unique to the South, either. Most Northern whites felt the same way. Northerners may have fought to bring about an end to slavery, but the majority were not prepared to accept blacks as equals. Such a racial prejudice was typically justified in ways that seem appalling to modern Americans. An example is found in the words of Benjamin F. Perry, who was appointed by President Andrew Johnson as the provisional governor of South Carolina in 1865:

 ## THE ORIGIN OF "JIM CROW"

For the modern reader, the term "Jim Crow" is synonymous with the laws created in the United States during the last decades of the nineteenth century. They were designed to institute segregation into the daily lives of blacks and whites. Social contact had not been generally discouraged between the races prior to the 1880s, but lawmakers ensured that the races remained apart by segregating everything from public inns to public transportation.

Why the name "Jim Crow" for these early segregation laws? The answer is unclear, but the origins of the term "Jim Crow" are fairly well documented. The reference "Jim Crow" dates back to about 1830. At that time, minstrel shows were a popular staple of entertainment for white audiences in both the North and the South. In a typical minstrel show, white performers would put on makeup to simulate the appearance of black Americans. Their performances would include music associated with black people and songs and lively dancing. Wearing "blackface" makeup, such white performers would often mimic black performers by using stereotypes.

One such blackface performer was a Northern white actor named Thomas "Daddy" Rice who performed in minstrel shows during the 1830s and 1840s. Rice blackened his face with charcoal paste or burnt cork and performed a kinetic, crazy dance mocking blacks to a popular song titled "Jump Jim Crow." According to legend, Rice patterned his character after either a crippled and elderly black man he had seen or a lively black boy (he had visited the South on occasion). During the performance he had witnessed, the black performer sang a song that included the following

The African has been in all ages, a savage or a slave. God created him inferior to the white man in form, color, and intellect, and no legislation or culture can make him his equal. . . . His hair, his form, and features will not compete with the Caucasian race, and it is in vain to think of elevating him to the dignity of the white man.[10]

lines: "Weel about and turn about and do jis so, Eb'ry time I weel about I jump Jim Crow."* The image of a prancing, shuffling, silly black man on stage was just what many white audiences loved to watch.

According to some historians, Rice patterned his stereotyped stage figure on a slave he met who was owned by a man named Crow, which would also explain the name Jim Crow in the song Rice performed on stage. Regardless of its origins, however, by the 1850s, the term "Jim Crow" was a popular reference on the minstrel circuit and other performers did shows using the same racial stereotype.

Eventually, Jim Crow became a term denoting a racial slur with which to refer to blacks. There were variations, in name as well, including "Zip Dandies," which became a popular blackface character in minstrel shows. A "Zip Dandy" was a black character who wore loud, exaggerated clothes, including a tie and tails with a fancy top hat. Whereas Jim Crow images typically stereotyped rural Southern blacks, a Zip Dandy was meant to parody and mock urban blacks. The point of the stereotyped stage character was to "show how ridiculous blacks could be when they tried to ape the manners of white gentlemen."**

Even though historians have discovered the origins of Jim Crow as a character on the minstrel circuit of nineteenth-century America, it remains unclear just how the term came to be applied as a label for laws created to establish social segregation in America.

*Quoted in Ronald L. F. Davis, "Creating Jim Crow: In-Depth Essay," www.jim-crowhistory.org/history/creating2.htm
**Ibid.

Despite such racist views, the radical ideas of the Reconstruction–era Congress forced social and political change on
the South. Southerners soon came around and accepted federal
guidelines and laws recognizing black rights. By 1868, many of
the former Confederate states had fallen into line and rejoined
the Union. Near year's end, only three Southern states were
still under federal military control. The Fifteenth Amendment
was passed two years later, and the march on behalf of black
freedom continued to move forward. By then, the early 1870s,
the future of blacks in the South looked extremely promising.
There were still those who struggled against these political and
social efforts including the Ku Klux Klan, but the die on behalf
of black rights seemed cast.

In some respects, the challenge to expanded rights for
blacks did not evaporate during the early 1870s, but instead
took on more subtle aspects. Southerners sought ways to limit
black rights that did not immediately appear to violate federal
laws. For example, in 1871, officials in Georgia created the first
poll tax as a requisite for voting. The poll tax could be viewed
as nondiscriminatory toward blacks because it was not required
only of them but rather of all voters, regardless of race. The vast
majority of blacks were simply too poor to afford to pay the tax,
however, so they were often denied the vote.

There were other forms of protest against the effort to legally equalize blacks. Such efforts appeared to exist outside the
confines of the law. On a street level, racist whites treated blacks
as inferiors in everyday business and at social events. A white
innkeeper might refuse to allow a black family to rent a room
for a night. A storekeeper might deny service to blacks or wait
on whites before doing business with potential black customers.
Bankers might not allow blacks to do business with them. Cem-
eteries might be open only to whites. Schools, public transportation, and even churches might be closed to blacks. At every
turn, blacks might find obstacles lain down by whites to deny
them civil rights and freedom of movement.

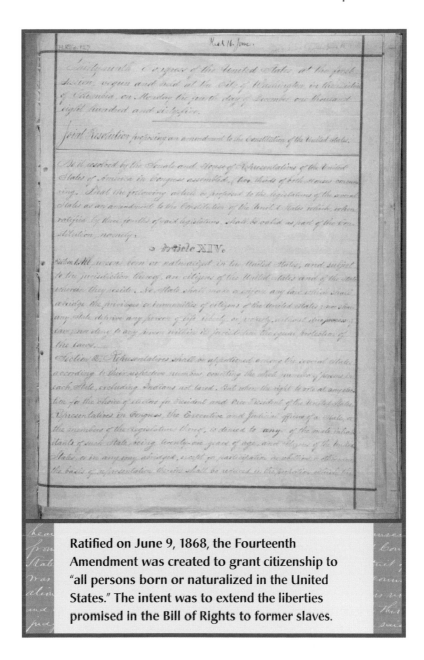

Ratified on June 9, 1868, the Fourteenth Amendment was created to grant citizenship to "all persons born or naturalized in the United States." The intent was to extend the liberties promised in the Bill of Rights to former slaves.

## THE CIVIL RIGHTS ACT OF 1875

In response to this continued discrimination, during the later years of Reconstruction, the U.S. Congress took one more step with the intent to protect black rights and guarantee they were recognized. This new legislation was yet another civil rights bill. When it received the vote of the majority of the Congress, the Civil Rights Act of 1875 came into existence. The law was sponsored by one of the longtime supporters of black rights, white Massachusetts Senator Charles Sumner. For decades, Sumner had championed the cause against slavery. During the years of Reconstruction, Sumner was a leading voice in support of black equality. He was one of the few Northerners to give support to the integration of schools, a position he supported more than a decade before the Civil War. Sumner died in 1874, before the legislation was fully passed.

The focus of the Civil Rights Act of 1875 was to plug the loopholes that were not covered by the Civil Rights Act of 1866. The new law stated "that all persons . . . shall be entitled to the full and equal enjoyment of the accommodations, advantages, facilities, and privileges of inns, public conveyances on land or water, theaters, and other places of public amusement."[11] For all the good intentions of the Congress, however, the days of Reconstruction were drawing to a close. Americans were tired of holding the South at arm's length, and many Southern states had been readmitted to the Union already. In the same year that the act became law, conservative white Democrats had regained power and control of their governments in many of the former states of the Confederacy. Also, many Americans, including many Northerners, had always been tepid in supporting the ever-expanding political and social rights of blacks.

In 1877, Reconstruction came to an official end. The Civil Rights Act of 1875 was never seriously enforced by the federal government. Then, in 1883, the U.S. Supreme Court nullified the law, declaring it unconstitutional. The majority of the court claimed that the act violated the power of the Fourteenth Amendment, which protected blacks from discrimination at the hands of state governments but not by private businesses or citizens. A new future seemed to loom for America's blacks.

# 2

# Redirecting Race

In 1877, the extended era of Reconstruction came to an end. Once federal agents and military personnel had left positions of authority and power, Southerners, with the backing of the federal government, stepped up and began to systematically dismantle the framework of safeguards and legal mandates that had been created since the war.

The status of blacks did not return to what it had been before the violent conflict between the North and the South. After all, slavery no longer existed, so blacks were no longer considered property. The U.S. Constitution contained three new amendments—the Thirteenth, Fourteenth, and Fifteenth—that

25

were designed to provide enfranchisement and citizenship for America's black population. Blacks were able to create their own worlds in which they lived in tightly knit family units that whites could not typically control. They built schools to educate their children, worshiped in their own churches, and helped fellow blacks through charities and benevolent societies. Blacks could become entrepreneurs, and some came to own property.

Reconstruction had not ended as a complete success on behalf of the advancement of black rights and freedoms, however: When it ended in 1877 and the last of the Republican state governments fell apart, many black leaders who held important public offices were pushed aside. As the black lieutenant governor of South Carolina, Robert Brown Elliot, resigned that same year, he spoke for more than just himself: "I desire to place on record, in the most public and unqualified manner, my sense of the great wrong which thus forces me practically to abandon rights conferred on me, as I fully believe by a majority of my fellow citizens of this State."[12] The day of black power over Southern politics was passing.

## DEMOCRATS RECLAIM THE SOUTH

By the late 1870s, white Democrat Southerners had regained power over state politics. Those same leaders ferreted out ways to negate and undermine black political power and its leaders. Sometimes these efforts constituted violence and intimidation, and they continued into the 1880s and 1890s. Many blacks who had voted in the days after the Civil War became so fearful of white reprisals, especially at the hands of the Ku Klux Klan, that they stopped voting and otherwise participating in politics. Such "street-level" efforts had a strong, negative impact on many blacks. But Southern leaders organized to keep nearly all blacks from voting through the enactment of poll taxes, literacy tests, and property qualifications. One such action was begun in South Carolina in 1882. The white-controlled state legislature passed the Eight Box Law, which was a form of literacy test. Any

This commemorative print marks the May 19, 1870, cel-ebratory parade for the Fifteenth Amendment in Baltimore, Maryland. The Fifteenth Amendment granted black men the right to vote.

black voters unable to read could not identify the appropriate boxes in which to place their ballots.

Each Southern state developed its own system of laws de-signed to restrict black voting. Such efforts had to be created carefully so as not to appear to violate the Fifteenth Amend-ment. When black leaders representing 40 Mississippi counties protested their state's "violent and criminal suppression of the black vote,"[13] the state's white leaders called for a constitutional convention with intentions to completely eliminate black vot-ing. When the convention was held (with only 1 black delegate and 134 whites), the delegates hammered together a set of voting requirements that did not mention blacks specifically but were intended to target black voters. Anyone voting in Mississippi was required to prove his residence in the state, to have all his taxes paid, and to have paid a two-dollar poll tax. In addition, anyone who had been convicted of the crimes of arson, bigamy, or even petty theft was disqualified from voting. These were considered "black" crimes. (Anyone who might have been convicted of murder, rape, or grand larceny, crimes then associated with whites, was allowed to vote.) Also, Mississippi law enacted a literacy test for voting—but the law allowed illiterate men to vote if they could interpret a section of the Constitution when it was read aloud to them. Determining whether a person understood the Constitution orally was left in the hands of white election officials and voting registrars who routinely accepted white would-be voters and rejected those who were black.

The results were obvious. Hundreds of thousands of blacks had gained the right to vote after the Civil War, but nearly all of them were soon without political enfranchisement. During the 1876 presidential election, nearly 100,000 black men in South Carolina alone had voted. By 1888, the number of black voters in that state had dropped to about 14,000. This number was still considered unacceptable to the majority of the state's whites, and a state constitutional convention was called in 1895. Using Mississippi law as their example, South Carolinians added their own "understanding clause" as a qualification for illiterate voters.

With such restrictive laws on the books, some whites were also losing their voting privilege because they were unable to pass literacy tests or pay poll taxes. In 1898, the state of Louisiana discovered a loophole that helped eliminate the possibility of whites being caught in the nonvoting net along with blacks. The new strategy came to be known as the "Grandfather Clause." Such clauses designated that only those who had been able to vote legally before 1867 could be allowed to vote. Those who did not fit into that category could still vote if their fathers or grandfathers had been able to vote. This eliminated nearly all black voters, because neither they nor their ancestors had been voters before 1867. During the 1890s, all Southern states except Kentucky and West Virginia enacted such laws. In the meantime, the federal government took few significant steps against such tactics designed to throw blacks out of the political process.

## THE SPREAD OF SEGREGATION

Additional laws were being created during the 1880s and 1890s to further restrict blacks. These laws established segregation of the races as the norm across the South. There had always been an understanding regarding the two races that blacks were inferior to whites, but interaction on a social level was common. In fact, the concept of segregation was almost foreign to American race relations in the South before the Civil War. Socially, the races had always mixed, even in the South. Laws did not restrict these interactions, even though social custom laid its own peculiar fences around how the races intermingled. Whites were busy ostracizing blacks from the political process across the South, but blacks were not generally restricted by law from rubbing shoulders with whites.

A case in point: During a visit to South Carolina in 1885, T. McCants Stewart, a black lawyer from New York, wrote about his trip. He had found his reception in the South hospitable and pleasant, with almost no signs of discrimination: "I can ride in first class cars on the railroads and in the streets. I can go into saloons and get refreshments even as in New York. I can stop in and drink a glass of soda and be more politely waited upon than in some parts of New England."[14] Stewart's trip to South Carolina took place before the development of segregation, designed by whites to restrict even social interaction of the races.

Before such laws, blacks and whites in the South interacted socially as they had for decades previously, when slavery generally provided the defining boundary of racial interaction. Before the arrival of codified legal restraints against the socialization of

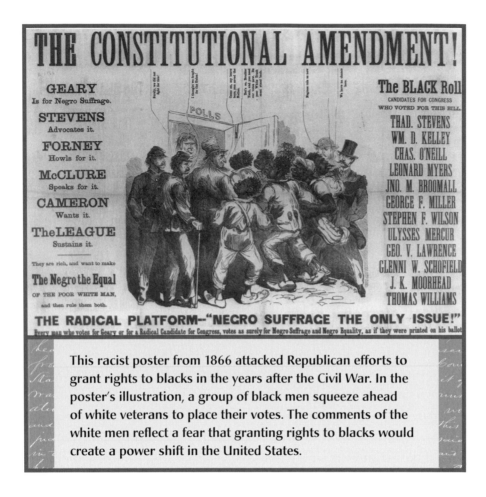

This racist poster from 1866 attacked Republican efforts to grant rights to blacks in the years after the Civil War. In the poster's illustration, a group of black men squeeze ahead of white veterans to place their votes. The comments of the white men reflect a fear that granting rights to blacks would create a power shift in the United States.

blacks and whites, the contact between them could be nearly color blind. Historian Edward L. Ayers described this preseg-regationist South:

> Few laws circumscribed day-to-day rural race relations. Rural roads, country stores, and cotton gins were not segregated; hunters and fishermen respected rules of fair play, regardless of race. Corn shuckings saw black and white men working around the same fire and black and white women cooking over the same food, though members of the two races went to separate tables when it came time to eat. In the diary of Nannie Stillwell Jackson, a white Arkansas

woman of moderate means, it is difficult to determine whether the people she describes are white or black. Jackson tells, with affection and gratitude, of the visits and gifts black friends brought her during an illness. She trades with her black neighbors, writes and receives letters for them, sews for them; a black midwife tends to her baby. The best of Southern race relations appeared in such scenes, where individuals developed personal respect for one another beyond the reach of hateful laws. The conditions of the New South, though, often worked against people of good will, whatever their race.[15]

During the 1880s and 1890s, racial integration was taking place on several fronts, not by law but by custom.

Even as the races found ways to make connections and contact in daily life, there was always a subtext, an unspoken understanding that blacks were inferior. As white Southerner Harry Crews remembered of his childhood and the time he spent growing up alongside his black friends, "There was a part of me in which it did not matter at all that they were black. But there was another part of me in which it had to matter because it mattered to the world I lived in."[16]

After the Civil War, whites, "in a quest to channel the relations between the races,"[17] began to create laws to divide the races. From Reconstruction on, most Southern institutions, including schools, courthouses, hospitals, poorhouses, orphanages, and even insane asylums were segregated. Perhaps a majority of white-operated hotels, inns, and restaurants did not provide services to blacks. Even churches "quickly broke into different congregations for blacks and whites."[18] There were other places off limits to blacks, although not officially. Many blacks in the South simply understood "not [to] venture where they felt unwelcome or where they were likely to meet hostility."[19]

The result of these legal and social changes can be read in the words of a Memphis newspaper editorial published in 1885:

# "SMOKING CARS" AND "PARLOR CARS"

At the center of the issue of access to railroad accommodations were the types of passenger cars available on both Southern and Northern lines. During the last decades of the 1800s, American railroads generally operated two types of passenger service: first class and second class. Who rode which was based on some perhaps surprising criteria. Typically, first-class cars carried women and men who did not smoke tobacco, whereas those who rode second-class or "smoking cars" were "men who chewed or smoked, men unaccompanied by women, and people who could not afford a first-class ticket."* As a result, the majority of second-class passengers were men whose behavior was certainly less than exemplary:

> The floors were thick with spit and tobacco juice, the air thick with smoke and vulgarities. The second-class car had hard seats, low ceilings, and no water; frequently, it was merely a part of the baggage car set off by a partition. The second-class car ran right behind the engine, and was often invaded by smoke and soot. The cars saw more crowding of strangers than in any other place in the [post–Civil War] South. "The cars were jammed, all the way over here, with the dirtiest, nastiest set I ever rode with," a Louisiana man complained about a trip to Texas.**

In comparison, a first-class passenger car, often called a "parlor car," provided transportation for a different class of people. The cars were clean, the seats were overstuffed and plush, and the floor was covered not with tobacco juice but with an elegant carpet. Sometimes, coolers dispensed ice water. Those onboard such cars might be a varied group of passengers, including blacks, but "their behavior tended to be more genteel than those in the smoking car."***

Not everyone across the South was prepared to accept black passengers in first-class rail cars, regardless of their class, money, or status. Sometimes, prior to segregation laws, even if a black person had purchased a first-class ticket, white passengers and even some train conductors would not allow him or her to enter the first-class car. He or she was forced into the second-class car instead. In 1889, a group from the First African Baptist Church of Savannah, led by a minister named Emmanuel Love, found this out the hard way. The group bought first-class tickets to ride a train from Savannah to a religious convention in the Northern city of Indianapolis.

As the party of black men and women traveled the line, word was telegraphed ahead and, during a stop at a depot in Georgia, the group was assaulted by a mob of at least 50 white men brandishing hand-guns, clubs, and iron rods, intent on removing the black passengers from their lawful seats. One man pointed a pistol at a frightened black woman, Mrs. Janie Garnet, a schoolteacher and graduate of Atlanta University. As she screamed in terror, her assailant stuck the weapon in her chest and shouted to her: "You G-d d-d heffer, if you don't hush your mouth and get out of here, I will blow your G-d d-d brains out."[†] The party had to be treated for broken bones and finished the trip to Indianapolis in a separate car. Ironically, before buying his party's tickets, Reverend Love had expected his party to ride in such a car "so they would not antagonize white first-class passengers who might be on board."[††]

---

[*]Quoted in Edward L. Ayers, *The Promise of the New South: Life After Reconstruction*. New York: Oxford University Press, Inc., 1992, p. 136.
[**]Ibid.
[***]Ibid.
[†]Ibid., p. 316.
[††]Ibid. p. 138.

"The colored people make no effort to obtrude themselves upon the whites in the public schools, their churches, their fairs, their Sunday-schools, their picnics, their social parties, hotels or banquets. They prefer their own preachers, teachers, schools, picnics, hotels and social gatherings."[20] An ever increasing number—hundreds and hundreds—of these "Jim Crow Laws" were passed by state legislatures.

## RAILROAD SEGREGATION

Although blacks and whites could and did restructure their common interaction after Reconstruction, there was one means by which they came together that was difficult to change by habit or practice: public transportation, a relatively new phenomenon in America. During the nineteenth century, both Northern and Southern American cities grew rapidly. Between 1840 and 1860, for example, New York City's population grew from 300,000 to 800,000, a 167 percent increase in just 20 years. As their urban landscapes spread and streets became crowded with people, the cities developed common means of public transport. In earlier decades of the nineteenth century, "mass transit" took the form of stagecoaches called omnibuses and small horse-drawn wagons. During the later decades of the nineteenth century, additional means of conveyance were streetcars, both horse drawn and electrical, as well as subways. Outside the urban centers, Americans needed to travel long distances and used steamboats and railroads. Such popular public means of transportation often put blacks and whites together. Some, especially those who did not want to see the races making regular equalized contact, came to believe that such public conveyances should be as segregated as all other public places.

Separation of the races on trains, streetcars, steamboats, and the like was not as simple as segregating hotels and theaters, however. Blacks may not have been happy being excluded from such white-run businesses, but "they could usually find, and often preferred, accommodations in black-run businesses."[21] It

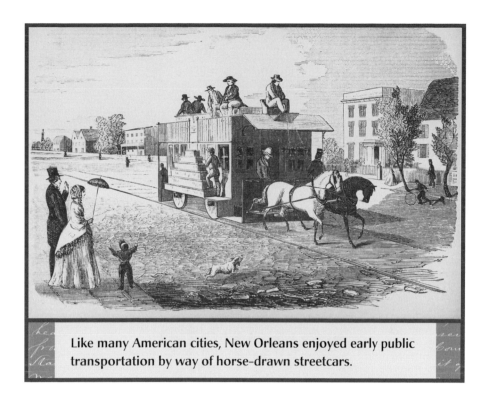

Like many American cities, New Orleans enjoyed early public transportation by way of horse-drawn streetcars.

was not as easy for blacks to find other means of transportation if denied access to those used by whites. Railroads were intended for use by the entire public, black and white, but as railroads expanded their services, especially after the Civil War, connecting Northern lines with Southern lines, problems developed:

> As the number of railroads proliferated in the 1880s, as the number of stations quickly mounted, as dozens of counties got on a line for the first time, as previously isolated areas found themselves connected to towns and cities with different kinds of black people and different kinds of race relations, segregation became a matter of statewide attention.[22]

EQUAL·JUSTICE·UNDER·LAW·

# 3

# Separate, but Equal

The problem of the races and public access to transportation emerged even before the Civil War. Separate car laws were enacted as early as 1841 in Massachusetts. After the war, Southern states led the way in establishing such laws. Some of these new laws were reminiscent of the Black Codes that already restricted the lives of blacks newly freed from slavery's bonds. In 1865, the legislature of Mississippi, while still in the hands of white legislators, passed a law that forbade "any freedman, Negro, or mulatto, to ride in any first class passenger cars, set apart, or used by and for white persons."[23] Although the law made it clear that blacks were not to ride in first-class cars, it did not establish completely separate cars for blacks. The law assumed that blacks and whites would mingle in second-class cars. The law was a model for other Southern states, such as Texas.

Three years later, Texas passed a law that established completely separate cars for black and white riders. There would be no opportunity for the two races to come in contact with one another. The law even stipulated that special cars be set

This 1856 engraving shows a freedman being expelled by a railroad conductor as a sympathetic Quaker mother looks on.

aside by the state's railroad companies to accommodate newly freed slaves. Texas's separate car law applied to all railroads operating within the state. These early laws did not remain in place. Once Texas and other Southern states were forced to accept Reconstruction government, the new legislators, many of whom were black, immediately worked to remove them from the books.

During the 1870s, the issue of separate car laws did not die, but the nature of the discussion shifted somewhat. Earlier laws had targeted blacks, making it difficult for them to gain access to first-class railroad passenger cars, but some Southerners, especially those of upper-class and monied interests, seemed more concerned that they were sharing first-class rides with lower-class whites whose behavior might be offensive or otherwise unacceptable. Some whites were prepared to accept a cultured, well-behaved, well-dressed black man as a fellow passenger rather than an uncouth white. As one Charleston newspaper editorialized, "To speak plainly, we need, as everybody knows, separate cars or apartments for rowdy or drunk white passengers far more than Jim Crow cars for colored passengers."[24] The result was that blacks and whites did share first-class accommodations on a regular basis. Such a scene surprised one English tourist in America when, in 1879, he rode Southern railroads and observed how "the humblest black rides with the proudest white on terms of perfect equality and without the smallest symptom of malice or dislike on either side."[25]

## THE CONCEPT OF "SEPARATE BUT EQUAL"

With the demise of Reconstruction and federal protections close at hand across the South, Jim Crow laws spread rapidly. The public transportation question led states to establish laws that regulated blacks' access to conveyances such as streetcars and railroads. The result was a curious alliance between "those who were genuinely concerned with fairness toward what they considered to be the inferior race" and "white supremacists, who feared further controls on the South."[26] In searching for a way to keep the races apart on various means of transportation without clearly supporting a social structure that trumpeted the concept of black inferiority, Southerners furthered the concept of "separate but equal." The concept managed to give nearly everyone a system that did not appear blatantly racist. Blacks and whites would be able to use the various systems of transport without having to come in close contact with one another. Whites could have their railcars; blacks could have cars of their own that would be the same as the cars used by whites. Many Southerners considered the idea a means for whites to meet blacks halfway.

In 1881, Tennessee was the first Southern state to use the concept of "separate but equal" in devising its system of transportation. Other states soon passed their own "separate but equal" laws. Florida came next, then Mississippi, Texas, and North Carolina. Florida's law appeared even more "generous" than Tennessee's. Its additional wording included the phrase "no white person shall be permitted to ride in a Negro car or to insult or annoy Negroes in such car."[27]

## OPPOSITION TO "SEPARATE BUT EQUAL"

As these laws were being written, redefining the interaction between the races, blacks did not support them. Regardless of how much the laws appeared to accommodate blacks, one underlying truth could not be ignored for long. These laws generally were created for one reason: It was a seemingly civilized way to practice segregation and to remind blacks that they were considered so inferior that whites did not want to share a public means of transportation with them.

Some blacks at first welcomed the passage of "separate but equal" laws, but it did not take long before the true intent of such laws became clear. It also became clear that the phrase "separate but equal" meant nothing to whites, who took only the aspect of "separate" seriously. Blacks discovered that there would never be an attempt by whites to create dual systems that would truly be "equal." The passenger cars on trains, as well as on other means of conveyance divided between whites and blacks, were never equal. As Booker T. Washington, a black leader of the late nineteenth century, noted of the cars provided for blacks on Southern railroads, "In every one of the Gulf states, the Negro is forced to ride in railroad coaches that are inferior in every way to those given the white, and they are made to pay the same fare as whites."[28]

The result of this unbalanced access to public transportation soon led blacks to oppose the concept of "separate but equal." They knew that the sole purpose of such laws was to twist other laws to suit the wants of whites or to skirt around such laws completely. With the passage of each new law that promised separation but equality, the message of racist whites was driven further home.

Blacks were not the only ones who did not like the new "separate but equal" laws. They were joined by the railroad companies themselves. Many of the rail companies were Northern companies that served Southern destinations, and the mindset of these companies did not parallel the blatantly segregationist policies. Also, simply from a business standpoint, all "separate but equal" laws that required different passenger cars for blacks and whites added to the cost of doing business. At a minimum, these laws required the railroads to provide at least four passenger cars per train: separate first-class and smoking cars for whites and the same for blacks. This doubled the minimum number of cars that the railroads might need for a train. Railroads chafed under these laws, especially when they had to put four cars on a train that was not a major line—one that did not have a large number of passengers. Several of the cars might run nearly empty, especially those designated for blacks, because not many blacks could afford to ride on the railroads. In some places, railroads defied the laws and did not provide separate cars for blacks and whites. This was done on

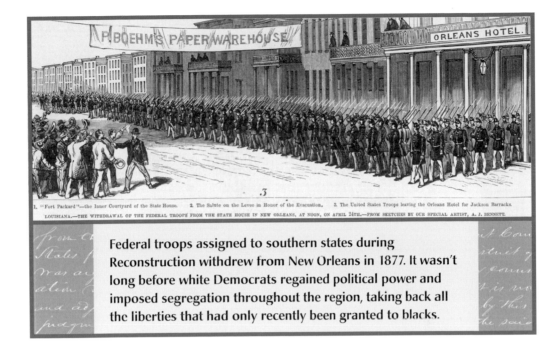

1. "Fort Packard"—the Inner Courtyard of the State House.    2. The Salute on the Levee in Honor of the Evacuation.    3. The United States Troops leaving the Orleans Hotel for Jackson Barracks.
LOUISIANA.—THE WITHDRAWAL OF THE FEDERAL TROOPS FROM THE STATE HOUSE IN NEW ORLEANS, AT NOON, ON APRIL 24TH.—FROM SKETCHES BY OUR SPECIAL ARTIST, A. J. BENNETT.

Federal troops assigned to southern states during Reconstruction withdrew from New Orleans in 1877. It wasn't long before white Democrats regained political power and imposed segregation throughout the region, taking back all the liberties that had only recently been granted to blacks.

a limited basis in few places: Although they did not like the demands placed on them by "separate but equal" laws, railroads could not afford to offend whites and involve state officials who might investigate noncompliance.

In most places across the South, blacks had few choices but to abide by the laws and accept their situation. Once white Southerners regained control of their states after Reconstruction, they held the power to keep blacks from effective protest. This was not the case everywhere, however: One exception was the city of New Orleans, because of the unique nature of race relations in the Crescent City and the profile of many of the city's blacks.

## SEGREGATION REACHES LOUISIANA

New Orleans was a city with a large mixed black population. Almost from the city's origins, its dominant minority was Creole, those of both black and French ancestry. This intermingling— typically between "Frenchmen and light-skinned women from French colonies in the Caribbean"[29]—dated back to the eighteenth century, when the French established their outpost settlement at the mouth of the Mississippi River. Over the

# THE SOUTH'S FIRST SEPARATE CAR LAW

Although the *Plessy v. Ferguson* case would come to center around the issue of whether a state government had the power to create separate car laws based on the concept of "separate but equal," Louisiana was not the first state to have such a law. In 1881, Tennessee became the first Southern state to pass such a statute. A law that called for public systems such as streetcars and trains to "furnish separate cars, or portions of cars cut off by partition wall, which all colored passengers who pay first class rates of fare may have the privilege to enter and occupy"* was passed. The white legislators who created the dualistic law felt that they had accommodated black passengers without embarrassing or belittling them.

At first, blacks reacted with enthusiasm, accepting such laws as generous. They knew, after all, the difficulties they regularly faced when attempting to purchase first-class tickets. Even if ticket agents sold them the tickets they wanted, they often were mistreated by fellow passengers or denied seating by conductors and other railroad officials. Also, blacks were accustomed to accepting inferior accommodations, schools, and general treatment at the hands of whites in other areas of life. Laws that promised them separate and equal facilities appeared to represent a step up from the norm. In time, however, black Southerners would come to feel differently about such laws. Each actually represented a step backward, another effort to keep blacks from entering the mainstream of American society.

*Quoted in C. Vann Woodward, *The Strange Career of Jim Crow*, New York: Oxford University Press, 1957, p. xvi.

decades, New Orleans society had included much interaction between the races, with few restrictions placed on the movement of blacks. The city's black population, including Creoles, had always "enjoyed freedoms and privileges not available to blacks in most areas of the South."[30]

Almost all of the Creole population of New Orleans was free individuals. According to the 1810 census, the first taken after the purchase of Louisiana by the American government, the number of free Creoles stood at approximately 7,500. Thirty years later, the number had increased to more than 25,000. By 1860, however, the Creole population had dropped to 18,000. The causes for this seeming decline have been attributed to two factors: One was the emigration of Creoles out of the region, including moving abroad. The other is that thousands of Creoles were so light-skinned that they were able to pass for white and blend into the white population without detection. "Passing" for white had its own incentives. During the same decades that witnessed a seeming decline in New Orleans's Creoles—1840–1860—white legislators in Louisiana were passing laws intended to restrict the freedom of movement and opportunity for the state's free blacks. These laws included restrictions on owners freeing their slaves and bans on free blacks immigrating into Louisiana from other states. Additional measures were designed to discourage free blacks from remaining in Louisiana. With these pressures bearing down on them, Creoles who could pass for white began doing so.

These laws had a limited long-term impact. By 1861, Louisiana had seceded from the Union and joined the Confederate States. When the war ended, all 11 Confederate States had been defeated. For about three years, Louisiana struggled to emerge from its war losses and return to the fold of the Union. On June 25, 1868, a little more than three years after the end of the Civil War, the former Confederate State of Louisiana was allowed admittance back into the United States. Just days later, the people of Louisiana accepted the Fourteenth Amendment to the Constitution, which granted equal protection under the law to blacks. The law was fundamental in bringing about change in the newly readmitted Southern state, for more than a decade, the U.S. Supreme Court decision *Dred Scott v. Sandford* had served as the law of the land, denying citizenship to America's black population.

Over the next four years, additional laws, including the Fifteenth Amendment and the Civil Rights Act of 1870 (Enforcement Act), were created, all designed to protect blacks, not only in Louisiana, but in all states in the Union as well. The following year, the U.S. Congress passed the Enforcement Act of 1871 (popularly known as the Ku Klux Klan Act), which established the procedures and means by which black voting rights would be protected. The act also authorized the president of the United States to use military troops to guarantee that the rights of

The Republican governor of Louisiana from 1872–1873, Pinckney Benton Stewart (P.B.S.) Pinchback was the first African American to become a state governor.

even a single individual were not trampled. This trend on behalf of protecting an ever-expanding list of black freedoms, including citizenship and voting privileges, continued into the next year, when a black man, P.B.S. Pinchback, who had been serving as the Louisiana's lieutenant governor, became the first black governor in American history.

Across Louisiana and the city of New Orleans, blacks fully accepted these political and legal changes that dramatically altered their lives. After all, such laws ensured that blacks would find themselves at the center of Louisiana politics. Many residents of the state were black, constituting a significant block of voters. In the city of New Orleans alone, by the end of the 1870s, black males headed four of every five families. Many of these men encouraged their children to take advantage of the new opportunities afforded to Louisiana blacks by attending school, often for the first time. Education seemed to embody the future of Louisiana's young black population. One Louisiana Presbyterian minister, Reverend Thomas Calahan, wrote of this new era of black opportunity:

> Go out in any direction, and you meet negroes on horses, negroes with oxen, negroes on foot, . . . men, women, and children, negroes in uniform, negroes in rags; all hopeful, everyone pleading to be taught, willing to do anything for learning. They are never out of our rooms, and their cry is for "Books! Books!" And "when will school begin?"[31]

Schools were soon integrated throughout New Orleans. The future for blacks in Louisiana's parishes looked promising politically, socially, and educationally.

# 4 The Separate Car Bill

There were those who did not wish for Louisiana's blacks to gain rights so readily. Violence sometimes racked the streets of New Orleans as blacks were killed by mobs and rioters. In an effort to counter these rougher white elements, a new group was formed in 1873. The Unification Movement was organized by P.G.T. Beauregard, a Creole veteran of the Civil War and one of the most famous Confederate generals, and C.C. Antoine, Louisiana's black lieutenant governor, who had served as a captain in the Louisiana Colored Infantry of the Union Army, a black unit. These two veterans of the war, men who had fought on opposite sides, formed the Unification Movement with the purpose to "advocate by speech, and pen, and deed, the equal and impartial exercise by every citizen of Louisiana of every civil and political right guaranteed by the constitution and the laws of the United States."[32] At its meetings, the Unification Movement displayed a banner reading "Equal Rights, One Flag, One Country, One People."[33] The group would include many of the most important civic leaders in New Orleans. Among its first members was Homer Plessy's stepfather.

Over the years, the Unification Movement met with only limited success with its broad-based, open-minded agenda. Another organization would take its place several years later, arriving just in time to mount the charge against one of Louisiana's first "separate but equal" laws. The American Citizens' Equal Rights Association, or ACERA, had a credo similar to that of the Unification Movement: to "better secure the free and full exercise of every political and civil right as guaranteed to the American citizen by the constitution and laws of this government."[34] Drawn together with support from both blacks and whites, ACERA became the dominant force battling new laws such as restrictions on interracial marriage and segregated railroad cars. ACERA and its off-shoot organization, the Citizens' Committee, established formally in September 1891, led opposition to the Separate Car Act of 1890.

## BLACK RIGHTS AFTER THE WAR

With the coming of the Civil War and the Northern-controlled government of Reconstruction during the 1860s and 1870s, blacks and Creoles in Louisiana once again tasted freedom. The unique environment for blacks in New Orleans continued for years after not only the Civil War, but also after Reconstruction; it was a city where unrestricted movement for the Creole population remained relatively intact. Even by the 1880s, when other parts of the South were creating elaborate webs of Jim Crow laws and other legal restrictions for blacks, Louisiana remained behind the curve. As late as 1888, half of Louisiana's registered

Canal Street in New Orleans, shown here in 1870, was a bustling thoroughfare, overrun with pedestrians, streetcars, and horse-drawn wagons.

voters were black, and the state's legislature included 18 black members. Railroad cars and streetcars were still shared by blacks and whites alike. One out of every four residents was "officially" black. The city was quite open about race. Relations between blacks and whites were acceptable to many. In 1884–1885, when New Orleans hosted a world's fair, the World Cotton Centennial, the grand celebration was integrated. When one Northerner attended the fair, he was surprised at what he saw: "White and colored people mingled freely, talking and looking at what was of common interest." He was amazed to see that blacks "took their full share of the parade and the honors." To this unaware Northern visitor, blacks and whites in New Orleans appeared to share "an unconscious equality of privileges."[35]

With the arrival of a new decade, the 1890s, the relationship between blacks and whites in Louisiana was about to change. For years prior to 1890, other Southern states had systematically restricted their black populations through Jim Crow laws. These laws began to find their way into Louisiana.

In 1890, the state of Louisiana began to consider its own "separate but equal" law regarding railroad passenger cars. A New Orleans newspaper editorialized that the interracial interaction on a railcar was so significant that it demanded a separation of the races. In one editorial, the newspaper noted how "one is thrown in much closer communication in the [railroad passenger] car with one's traveling companions than in the theatre or restaurant," places that were already segregated by law.[36] In such cars, passengers are "crowded together, squeezed close to each other in the same seats, using the same conveniences, and to all intents and purposes in social intercourse."[37]

## THE LOTTERY AND SEPARATE CARS

For several years, despite the trend across the South during the 1880s, Louisiana government leaders took almost no steps toward establishing "separate but equal" laws. In 1890, however, the Louisiana legislature established the state's Separate Car Law. What caused the change and provided a different sort of motivation for this law is a story unique to Louisiana and New Orleans.

Throughout the nineteenth century, New Orleans had become the South's prevailing symbol as "the region's wayward sister."[38] The city was a crossroads of river traffic, linking the Mississippi River watershed with the Gulf of Mexico, and an important international port. The Crescent City was home to many drinking establishments (650 saloons altogether), breweries, red-light districts, and gambling houses. In 1890, the Louisiana legislature was considering a law that would ban "all dance houses, free and easy gambling dens, barrel houses, and shandangoes."[39]

In addition to this proliferation of questionable establishments in and around New Orleans, for some, there was another sign of the city's and the state's immorality: the Louisi-

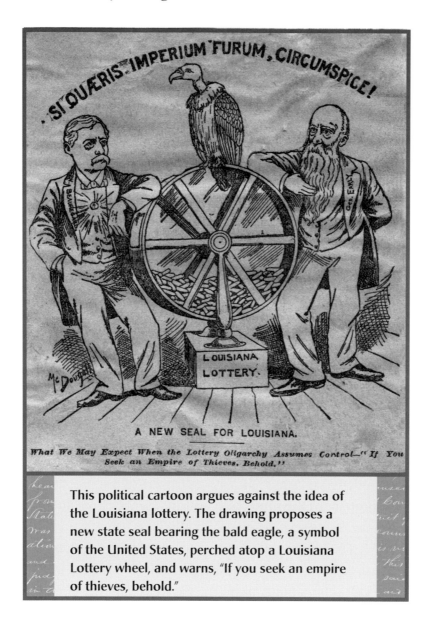

SI QUÆRIS IMPERIUM FURUM, CIRCUMSPICE!

LOUISIANA LOTTERY.

A NEW SEAL FOR LOUISIANA.

*What We May Expect When the Lottery Oligarchy Assumes Control—"If You Seek an Empire of Thieves, Behold."*

This political cartoon argues against the idea of the Louisiana lottery. The drawing proposes a new state seal bearing the bald eagle, a symbol of the United States, perched atop a Louisiana Lottery wheel, and warns, "If you seek an empire of thieves, behold."

ana Lottery Company, which was one of the most lucrative in the country. Created in 1868 by the Louisiana legislature, the lottery was a multimillion-dollar business. Many of the city's residents participated in the lottery, and more than 100 shops were scattered around the city just to sell tickets. Lottery tickets weren't cheap—$20 each—but the lure to participate in the lottery was great because the company held monthly drawings with as much as $300,000 going to a lucky winner. So many people played the lottery that the city's moralists constantly criticized the system for encouraging a high level of gambling in New Orleans. In May 1890, Louisiana Governor Francis T. Nicholls gave a speech in which he spoke against the Louisiana Lottery Company, referring to the lottery as "gambling of the very worst description."[40] He called for an end to it.

In 1890, the year of the Separate Car Law, the 25-year lease for the lottery was coming close to expiration. In the face of criticism from Governor Nicholls, the company was desperate for the lottery to be rechartered and sought an amendment to the state constitution that could be voted on by the people. As the issue came before the legislature, it created a firestorm, splitting both the Republican and Democratic parties into pro-lottery and anti-lottery camps.

As the new lottery bill circulated in the legislature, another bill, one that called for the institutionalization of "separate but equal" railroad cars, was also making its way around. It was introduced in the legislature as House Bill #42, "an act to promote the comfort of passengers in railway trains."[41] The proposed bill, if passed, would require all railroads operating in Louisiana to provide different cars for blacks and whites. All those who violated the act would be subject to a $25 fine or 20 days in jail in the Orleans Parish Prison. For railroads that did not cooperate, the fine would be $500. Any railroad official who did not comply and enforce the act could be fined up to $50 for each offense.

The bill was proposed by Representative Joseph St. Amant and was immediately controversial. As it was written, with no exceptions, blacks and whites would not be able to ride in the same cars. If an interracial married couple wanted to board the same train, the man and woman would have to ride in separate cars. The proposed law would require railroads to always provide cars for blacks, even if there were almost no regular black passengers.

Upon the bill's proposal in the legislature, ACERA sprang into action to oppose the legislation. On May 24, a delegation representing ACERA went to Baton Rouge, the Louisiana capital, to speak out against the proposed Separate Car Law. Two of those present in the delegation were James Lewis and Laurent Auguste, who had been members of the Unification Movement. In making their presentation to Louisiana's lawmakers, ACERA members made their position clear: "We do not think that citizens of a darker hue should be treated by law on different lines than those of a lighter complexion. Citizenship is national and has no color. We hold that any attempt to abridge it on account of color is simply a surrender of wisdom to the appeals of passion."[42] When one legislator attempted to add an amendment to the bill that would allow a white person's servants to ride in a whites-only car, a black legislator chastised him, reminding his colleague that this amendment would allow black servants to ride in white cars but would not allow him, a state legislator, to do so.

## LEGISLATIVE STRUGGLE

Debate raged in the Louisiana House of Representatives. Finally, the House voted 56 to 23 to send the measure to the Senate. Both the lottery issue and the proposed separate car legislation landed in the Senate at the same time. Some legislators who opposed the separate car bill hoped that the lottery issue would consume most of their time, leaving the car bill to languish. Despite much debate, the lottery issue came to a vote with the Senate deciding 24 to 12 in favor of a new lottery. The governor soon threatened to veto the bill, however.

In the meantime, with only ten days left in the legislative session, the issue of the separate car bill was resurrected. It is believed that Senator Murphy Foster, the powerful president pro tempore who was staunchly anti-lottery, "resurrected the Separate Car Act as punishment to only the black legislators who supported the lottery."[43]

Throughout the following week, a dual drama unfolded in the Louisiana legislature. The governor vetoed the lottery issue, but the House overturned him by a vote of 66 to 31. The showdown between the governor and the Senate did not pan out, however, because pro-lottery senators realized that they did not have enough votes to override the governor. Instead, they insisted that the governor did not have the authority to

Murphy Foster served as both a state senator and governor of Louisiana. Foster brought back the Separate Car Act in response to aggressive lottery legislators.

veto an amendment to the Louisiana constitution. When the Senate's judiciary committee agreed (most of the committee's members were pro-lottery men), the lottery was advanced to be placed on the ballot for the people to vote on. The push-pull over the future of the lottery was decided two years later,

## THE *CRUSADER*: NEW ORLEANS'S NEWSPAPER FOR BLACKS

Although New Orleans was not a typical Southern city in terms of race relations, during the 1880s and 1890s, the Crescent City was not completely tolerant or accepting of its black or Creole population. The city's white-owned and white-operated newspapers often wrote about its black populations with disdain, ridicule, and much condescending head patting. In 1889, Creole lawyer and doctor Louis A. Martinet decided that his fellow blacks needed a newspaper that spoke not only to them, but also for them. That year, he launched the *Crusader*. What a difference one newspaper can make.

The paper was published in Martinet's offices, located at 411 Exchange Alley in the city's French Quarter. From its first publication, the weekly paper, which was published on Saturdays, was intended to be "newsy, spicy, progressive, liberal, stalwart, and fearless."* From its inception and its first issues, the *Crusader* was the newspaper of New Orleans's black and Creole populations.

Its pages were filled with street-level interests, including sports scores. There were laudatory lists of high-school graduating classes and advertisements for everything from flags to cigars, violin lessons to first-communion wreaths, and "Mexican Mustang Liniment for Man and Beast."** Bulletins announced masquerade balls, church raffles, benefits on behalf of local widows, and "Christian entertainment." An announcement for the Co-operators Companions Debating Social Circle informed readers that "no lady will be admitted [to its picnic] without an invitation."***

when the people of Louisiana voted to continue the lottery for another 25 years.

The lottery company was pleased with the outcome of all the political horse trading between those who favored the lottery and those who opposed it, but those who opposed the

In addition to all these necessary and popular inclusions, the *Crusader* was also a "Republican journal," and its motto demanded "A Free Vote and Fair Count, Free Schools, Fair Wages, Justice and Equal Rights."[†] Thus, the paper's columns and editorials were constantly campaigning in print for the advancement of the rights of blacks not only in New Orleans, but also across the United States. Reporters informed readers about any acts of racial violence perpetrated against blacks, stories that did not generally make the pages of white-owned newspapers.

When the Separate Car Law was winding its way through the Louisiana legislature, the *Crusader* went into action in opposition to the "separate but equal" legislation. Martinet, who had served as a legislator during the 1870s, admonished the governor to veto the bill. He even sent a personal telegram to Nicholls: "Governor, thousands good and true men urge you to veto Separate Car Act."[††] The newspaper did not win the issue or the day. Despite opposition from the paper, which included many blacks and even some whites, Governor Nicholls signed the Separate Car Act into law on July 10, 1890.

[*]Quoted in Keith Weldon Medley, *We as Freemen: Plessy v. Ferguson.* Gretna, LA: Pelican Publishing Company, 2003, p. 104.
[**]Ibid., p. 106.
[***]Ibid., p. 105.
[†]Ibid., p. 106.
[††]Ibid., p. 104.

separate car bill were dealt a harsh blow. Eight white senators who either had voted against the separate car bill in an earlier vote or had been absent to avoid voting on the issue set their sights. Prepared to punish black legislators who had supported the lottery, these politicians turned on their black colleagues and voted against them and their race.

## RALLYING AGAINST THE SEPARATE CAR BILL

Despite the votes of both the Louisiana House and Senate in favor of the separate car bill, the legislation still needed the signature of the state's governor, Francis Nicholls. In the meantime, those opposed to the legislation bolted into action to crusade against the law that would relegate blacks to an official status of inferiority. To be sure, some blacks supported the law, including former Louisiana Governor P.B.S. Pinchback, who assured his fellow blacks that this law would serve as a guarantee that they would receive first-class treatment from the state's railroads. Many others, such as Rodolphe Lucien Desdunes, a black journalist from New Orleans, were unconvinced. Desdunes spoke out against the separate car bill, insisting to his readers that "it is more noble and dignified to fight . . . than to show a passive attitude of resignation."[44]

Others rallied and wrote against the bill. One of the most important was Louis A. Martinet, a Creole lawyer and doctor who had founded a political newspaper called the *Crusader* in 1889. This newspaper would speak on behalf of blacks. These protests fell on deaf ears: Nicholls signed the Separate Car Act into law on July 10, 1890.

Martinet did not surrender the issue even after the governor's decision and the establishment of the new law that would separate blacks and whites in one more arena. This view was reported in an editorial by Martinet in the *Crusader:*

Senator Murphy J. Foster is reported as having said that if
the colored senators had stood with his side as firmly against
the Lottery as they stood by it, he would have suffered his
body to be cut in pieces before he allowed the infamous car
bill to go through. . . . But the Senator has no right to inflict
a grievous wrong on the colored population of the State because a few colored Senators voted with the majority of the
white Senators.[45]

As Martinet concluded his critical editorial, he called for a
continuation of the struggle against the newly passed Separate
Car Act:

The next step is for the American Citizens' Equal Rights
Association to begin to gather funds to test the constitutionality of the law. We'll make a case, a test case, and bring
it before the Federal Courts on the ground of the invasion
of the right of a person to travel through the State unmo-
lested. No such case has been fairly made or presented. The
American Citizens' Equal Rights Association will make it, if
it understands its duty.[46]

Over the next two years, anti–separate car proponents
would doggedly pursue this single-minded goal.

·EQUAL·JUSTICE·UNDER·LAW·

# 5

# The Campaign Begins

L ouis Martinet's call for ACERA to lead the crusade to challenge the constitutionality of the newly passed Separate Car Act went largely unheeded. This organization would not take on the charge. ACERA had never become popular with many blacks, who thought that the group had not pursued its campaign against the Separate Car Act *before* its passage and did not have faith that it would do so *after* the bill had become law. Even Martinet came to feel that ACERA was not the proper organization to lead the fight, stating in a later editorial that "the proper men were not at the head" and that they would not rally around the cause except for personal advancement.[47]

## THE CITIZENS' COMMITTEE

It was not until September 1891 that another organization was formed to mount the fight against the Separate Car Act. By its very name, its cause was quite specific: The Citizens' Committee to Test the Constitutionality of the Separate Car Law. Among the ranks of this civil rights organization were various professionals, including teachers, businessmen, attorneys, former Union soldiers, government bureaucrats, and social activists. One committee member was a "jeweler and diamond setter" whose shop was just around the corner from Martinet's *Crusader* offices. A funeral home director and an undertaker were also members. Many of them came from New Orleans's elite population of free people of color who had never been slaves. Some were veterans of the old Unification Movement. The group included several important civic leaders among New Orleans's Creoles: Louis A. Martinet, Rodolphe Desdunes, Arthur Esteves, and C.C. Antoine.

President of the Citizens' Committee, which set out to fight Jim Crow laws, Creole sailmaker Arthur Esteves helped devise the idea to challenge the constitutionality of Louisiana's Separate Car Act.

Desdunes was a black writer who had editorialized against the Separate Car Act and for other black causes for years, sometimes in the pages of the *Crusader*. The group selected Esteves, a 56-year-old sailmaker as its president. Esteves had been one of the original members of the Unification Movement.

This passion-led collection of black and Creole leaders put their heads together and hammered out their strategy. At first, they considered organizing a boycott of all railroads within the state that required blacks to ride in separate cars. They soon switched to testing the segregation law altogether. Pursuing this tack would place the issue within the courts, and this would require money. The Citizens' Committee campaigned for funds and raised $3,000 for its legal fees; however, this amount would not begin to pay lawyers to take on a case intended to challenge the law's constitutionality. Such a legal battle might drag on for years and wind up before the United States Supreme Court.

Fortunately, Martinet had managed to locate an attorney from outside Louisiana who stepped in to provide legal counsel to the Citizen's Committee without payment. Albion Tourgée, a well-known white attorney originally from New York. Tourgée had served as a federal judge in North Carolina and had become quite vocal as an advocate of black rights. He had written about the legislative battle over the passage of the Louisiana Separate Car Act in a Chicago newspaper. Volunteering his services would be an important contribution to the campaign against the Jim Crow car act.

Tourgée intended to ride herd over the legal proceedings and provide legal expertise in the pursuit of a constitutional challenge. The Citizens' Committee still needed to find a Louisiana lawyer who would be willing to take the case. Even though the committee was based in New Orleans, a relatively free-thinking Southern city, very few white lawyers were willing to even consider taking on the committee's planned challenge of the Separate Car Act. A white lawyer named James C. Walker finally stepped forward. More than a year after the passage of the Separate Car Act, those opposed to the Jim Crow legislation were ready to directly mount a test case.

## FRAMING A TEST CASE

The Citizens' Committee was intent on putting the gears in motion on behalf of a test case against the Separate Car Act, but its members were uncertain how to go about it. They had to pick a means of questioning the act that would bring to court any and all of the issues that the committee wanted the legal system to consider. Knowing that white judges might be looking for any excuse to dismiss a case or decide against them, the members of the committee took their time. It became clear that the best way to bring a constitutional challenge to the Separate Car Act was to show how absurd the law was. The committee thought it would make the most sense to have someone—a black person, of course—violate the law by boarding the wrong car, but the legal challenge would have even more meaning if the violator would be a person of mixed race, one whose skin was so light that he or she could easily be mistaken for white. The committee considered having a light-skinned black woman board a whites-only railcar, thinking that she might receive more sympathy. Instead, they chose "a respectable, law-abiding, well-mannered, light-skinned black man."[48]

After making this decision, the committee had other details to work out. One concerned where their selected passenger would board a rail car. Some thought he should board in a neighboring state where there was no "separate but equal" law regarding railroad passengers and then ride that train into Louisiana—but all the states surrounding Louisiana had their own separate car laws. Thought was given to having their selected person board in a state distant from Louisiana, but the logistics of boarding in such a state, riding in an integrated car without being detected and arrested in a neighboring state, and winding up in Louisiana to be arrested were too complicated and questionable. Everything would have to fall exactly into place.

Finally, the committee members decided to have the person board a train in Louisiana.

There were additional concerns. Violence toward black railroad passengers was frequent. Before the passage of Louisiana's Separate Car Act, whites sometimes attacked blacks who boarded as first-class passengers even if they had first-class tickets. The committee certainly did not want their planned test case to result in violence, nor did they want their selected person to be placed in danger if it could be avoided. To that end, the Citizens' Committee decided to take the precaution of contacting local officials, including law officers and railroad personnel, to notify them of their plan. To keep word from leaking out to the wrong person, the committee decided to contact senior railroad officials. Even then, the plans of the committee met with resistance. After contacting officials of one Louisiana railroad, Martinet was told that they would not cooperate, that they were not going to arrest anyone, and that they did not even enforce the Separate Car Act. In making additional contacts, Martinet found that other railroads had the same policy. Officials for those railroads would typically post signs in their depots and stations that explained to would-be passengers which railcar they were to board according to their race. Once boarding began, however, officials and employees turned a blind eye. Martinet became frustrated. "The railroads are not in favor of the separate car law," he wrote, "owing to the expense entailed, but they fear to array themselves against it."[49]

In early 1892, however, Martinet managed to find one railroad in Louisiana that would cooperate with the Citizens' Committee. Officials of the Louisville and Nashville Railroad said that they would agree to arrest the passenger placed in one of their whites-only cars as long as their complicity was not made known to the public. Also, they demanded that, to make the whole event less controversial to whites, it would have to be a white person who actually filed the complaint against the light-skinned black passenger who boarded the L&N passenger car.

With a complete agreement struck between the railroad and the Citizens' Committee, the test case was ready for its trial run.

## CHALLENGING THE LAW

The committee selected one of its members to board a whites-only car on the L&N. Daniel Desdunes, the musician son of Rodolphe Desdunes was only one-eighth black. The younger Desdunes was provided a first-class ticket to ride on an L&N train on February 24, 1892. That morning, at eight o'clock, ticket in hand, Desdunes strode into a rail station along Canal Street in New Orleans. Before boarding the train, he was informed by rail officials that he would have to ride in the car reserved for black passengers. He refused. Instead, he climbed aboard a whites-only passenger car, destination Mobile, Alabama. The train left the station without incident. Then, as planned, the train's conductor approached Desdunes and informed him that he would have to leave the whites-only car and take a seat on the car reserved for blacks. Of course, Desdunes refused to cooperate. Two miles out, the conductor stopped the train at Elysian Fields and North Claiborne Avenues. At that point, Captain Edward Flood of the City Secret Service (who was another passenger in cooperation with the Citizens' Committee) signaled to a pair of men near the intersection. They were private detectives, also employed by the Citizens' Committee. They came onboard and arrested Desdunes, accusing him of having violated the Separate Car Act. No sooner had the detectives taken Desdunes to a local precinct station than the Citizens' Committee treasurer, Paul Bonseigneur, arrived and paid the bond for Desdunes's release. In the meantime, Captain Flood had sworn out an affidavit against Desdunes for violation of Act No. 111 of 1890—the Separate Car Law. Everything had gone according to plan.

During the months between Desdunes's arrest and his trial, the Citizens' Committee worked on its next strategy: how to present its case in court. The goal, after all, was not about Desdunes's fate, but about whether the Separate Car Act should remain the rule of law. Tourgée gave the committee a great deal of advice concerning how James Walker should approach and set the boundaries of the case before a judge. (Tourgée did not

# BLACK RIGHTS
# AND STAR CARS

The issue of segregation on public means of transportation was nothing new to blacks living in New Orleans when Homer Plessy began his odyssey in 1892. Decades earlier, just after the Civil War, blacks in the Crescent City had been segregated on an earlier form of transport, a slow-moving system of mule-driven streetcars called "star cars." Just as with the Plessy case, segretation with the star cars ignited protests from blacks.

In 1867, streetcars were a common means of mass transit in New Orleans. Approximately one of every three of these streetcars was marked with a large black star. This sign told would-be passengers that these cars were designated for black passengers. The only blacks exempt from the restriction were black veterans who had served in the Union Army during the war. Whites were not relegated to their own cars, however. The city's statutes allowed whites to board star cars when it was convenient for them. Blacks became increasing angered by this segregated and unfair system of city travel, and they eventually organized a protest in the form of, as one New Orleans newspaper stated, "a pre-concerted design on the part of a number of colored men."*

The protest took place on April 28, 1867. William Nicholls, a black man, boarded a whites-only car that bore no star. He argued with the car's driver and was soon arrested. With his actions, Nicholls had intended to be taken to court, where he could challenge the star car segregation policy, but the streetcar company refused to prosecute and instead dropped all charges. In case of a similar incident in the future, the streetcar company's officials decided to order their drivers to remain at a stop if a black passenger boarded a nonstarred car.

The company did not have to wait long for another incident to occur. On May 4, less than a week after Nicholls's attempt to chal-

come to New Orleans himself, sending his advice to the committee from out of state.) At the center of the strategic debate on procedure, committee members had wrestled with two

---

lenge the star car laws, another black man, Joseph Guillaume, organized a similar boarding. As reported in the newspaper, the *New Orleans Crescent*:

> The impending crisis was illustrated on Love St. [now North Rampart] at half past 11:00 yesterday morning in the Car No. 148 allotted for whites by the entrance of a dusky son of Africa, rejoicing in the name of Joseph Guillaume, who insisted upon riding therein. When remonstrated by the driver, he coolly took the rein in his own hands and was about transforming himself from a loyal citizen to a regular Jehu and a bruiser to anyone who dared to interfere with him.**

Guillaume's boarding of the nonstarred car took place just a block from the Plessy house.

Other incidents soon followed. Days later, a pair of black women boarded a nonstarred car and a black man took a seat on another whites-only car and got into an argument with a white passenger. Such incidents were taking place all over the city, constituting a citywide protest. Throughout that Sunday afternoon, multiple incidents took place. Hundreds of blacks gathered in the city's streets to support blacks who took seats on whites-only star cars. The following day, the streetcar companies across New Orleans began to eliminate the stars that designated cars for blacks.

---

*Quoted in Keith Weldon Medley, *We as Freemen: Plessy v. Ferguson*. Gretna, LA: Pelican Publishing Company, 2003, p. 79.
**Ibid.

Ignorance and neglect are
the mainsprings of misrule.
Albion W. Tourgee

Albion W. Tourgee, a famed novelist, Abolitionist, and lawyer, represent- ed Homer Plessy in his landmark Supreme Court case.

possible approaches. They could either claim that the Separate Car Act was unconstitutional because it violated the Fourteenth Amendment, which guaranteed due process and equal rights, or they could invoke the Interstate Commerce Act, both federal laws. Tourgée suggested that they use the Commerce Act because "the power of the federal government to regulate commercial travel between states had been solidly established."[50] The state- level Separate Car Act limited interstate travel by regulation and restriction, so it should be declared illegal. Tourgée's strategy did not stop there. He also suggested that the case include claims of state violation of the Thirteenth and Fourteenth Amendments. After all, the more federal issues the better. The case might one day land on the docket of the United States Supreme Court.

The judge appointed to hear Desdunes's case was Judge Robert Marr. Marr received documents filed by Walker on Des- dunes's behalf, claiming that the black passenger had been un- duly restrained in his right to travel. Walker argued that the state of Louisiana had no authority to intervene against Desdunes because rights of the road were protected by federal law. The

Separate Car Law constituted de facto racism because it "estab-
lishes an insidious distinction between Citizens of the United
States based on race which . . . abridges the privileges and immunities of Citizens of the United States . . . secured by the 13th
and 14th Amendments."[51] Desdunes's trial was interrupted that
April, when Judge Marr disappeared without a trace.

The case was suspended until the judge was found or replaced. Then, movement on the case began to unfold from different vantage points. In a separate case, the Louisiana Supreme
Court ruled on the Separate Car Act based on a decision in a
Texas case, *Abbot v. Hicks*. In that case, a Texas and Pacific Railway conductor was charged with violating the law by allowing a
black person to board a whites-only car. The conductor's attorney had argued his case on the same grounds that Tourgée had
suggested Walker used to argue Desdunes's case. The issue centered on whether the Texas separate car act constituted usurpa-
tion of federal power embodied in the Interstate Commerce Act.
The Texas court decided in favor of the railroad conductor. In
light of this decision, on May 25, the Louisiana Supreme Court
decided against the state's Separate Car Law, declaring it unconstitutional regarding trains that traveled from one state to another. The Desdunes case was dismissed because Desdunes had
boarded a train that was traveling from Louisiana to Alabama.

The Supreme Court's decision and the dismissal of Desdunes's case were greeted with great enthusiasm by blacks in
Louisiana in general and the Citizens' Committee specifically.
(Judge Marr's whereabouts had not been discovered in the in-
terim, and a judge named John Ferguson had been assigned to
the Desdunes case.) Martinet wasted no time noting his excite-
ment and feeling of victory in the pages of his *Crusader*: "The
Jim Crow car is ditched and will remain in the ditch. . . . The
young Professor Desdunes is to be congratulated on the manly
assertion of his right, and his refusal to ride in the Jim Crow
coach. The people should cherish the performance of such pa-
triotic acts and honor the patriots."[52]

The "victory" was only partially complete for the Citizens' Committee, however. Because Desdunes's case had not had its full hearing in court, the racial discrimination of the Separate Car Act had not been considered completely. In addition, the *Abbot v. Hicks* case in Texas had only established an issue regarding the clash of power and authority between state law and federal law. What about railroads that ran trains only within the borders of a single state, or intrastate travel?

## ANOTHER TEST CASE

With the Desdunes case having been thrown out by Judge Walker and the decision of a Texas court on a similar case, the future of the Separate Car Law regarding interstate travel was dead. The Citizens' Committee almost immediately moved forward with another test case, this time to defy the Separate Car Law regarding intrastate trains. Martinet set the stage in his editorializing:

> We have now to fight the Plessy case for our right to travel in the State. We need to reach a larger audience than can be reached in a few churches at one time—and then our agitation must be continued thereafter & not sporadic. . . . The people of the North must be educated to conditions in the South, & this can only be done through the press—and through our own press. . . . We must expose continually to the people of the North the hideous sores of the South & the ever-recurring outrages to which we are subjected & the lurking therein to the Nation.[53]

On June 7, 1892, just two weeks after the Louisiana Supreme Court's decision to strike down the Separate Car Act as unconstitutional in cases of interstate travel, Homer Plessy walked into a Louisiana railroad depot, boarded a whites-only car, and started the wheels turning on another test case.

The charge against Homer Plessy was "Violating Section 111 of the Separate Car Act." At the police station, Plessy did not

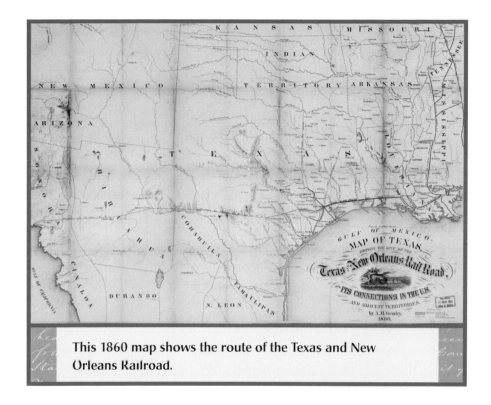

This 1860 map shows the route of the Texas and New Orleans Railroad.

find himself alone. Soon after his arrival at the Fifth Precinct station, he was joined by nearly half a dozen prominent members of the Citizens' Committee, including Rodolphe Desdunes and Louis Martinet. They were there as an act of support for Plessy and an act of defiance of Louisiana law.

Their plan to challenge the Separate Car Act regarding intrastate passenger service had unfolded with precision and clockwork. Nothing had interfered with their scheme that might have altered the intended outcome—no dramatic, unplanned confrontation had occurred between Plessy and the other passengers in the whites-only car, no violence had taken place, and no damage had been done to railroad property. After Plessy's arrest, the East Louisiana Railroad's Number Eight Train had steamed on and completed its otherwise routine trip to Covington, only without Homer Plessy. He had bought his first-class ticket without being questioned or raising suspicion, and the rest had happened as the Citizens' Committee had hoped. Plessy was still holding his ticket in his hand when he reached the police station.

His bond posted by the committee, Plessy went home that evening, only to return to court the following morning. He appeared before the Second Recorder's Court, located near New Orleans's St. Louis Cathedral, at 10:00 A.M. The court was presided over by A. R. Moulin, Judge First Recorder. Plessy was not the only one to appear that morning. The Number Eight Train's conductor, J.J. Dowling, was present, as were Detective Cain and a man named J.L. Mott, a witness to Plessy's actions. All three swore out affidavits that expressed the same sentiment, that Plessy had boarded the wrong passenger car and violated the Separate Car Law.

## OTHER ISSUES AT HAND

Soon, the story of Homer Plessy's defiance of the law was making the pages of Louisiana newspapers other than Martinet's *Crusader*. The New Orleans *Daily Crescent* prefaced one of its reports with the colorful, racially biased lines:

IN THE WRONG COACH
A Snuff-Colored Descendant of
Ham Kicks Against the "Jim"
Crow" Law
And Takes the Jail End of It Rather
Than Comply With Its Distinctive Provisions

Another paper, the *Daily Picayune*, was equally unsympathetic to Homer Plessy's defiant act and his subsequent arrest:

ANOTHER JIM CROW
CAR CASE
Arrest of a Negro Traveler
Who Persisted
In Riding With the White People

The case, which opened in the early summer of 1892 and continued along a four-year legal path, drew very little attention outside the immediate region affected by Homer Plessy's act of civil disobedience, however. Other issues were taking center stage at that time. Labor unions were struggling for membership and for their very existence as factory and railroad owners, usually supported by state officials, fought striking workers tooth and nail. That year, in Pennsylvania, national papers reported the bloodshed that took place at the Homestead steel mill outside Pittsburgh when workers fought Pinkerton detectives hired by the steel company to access the mills that the strikers had blocked. It was an election year that would once again pit Democratic candidate and former president Grover Cleveland against incumbent Republican Benjamin Harrison. A new political party was forming in America at that time, as well: the Populists, which formed as a grass-roots movement among the nation's farming interests and manufacturing workers. That year, they nominated their own candidate for president, James B. Weaver, who would poll a million votes in November.

There were other race-related issues in 1892. In particular that year saw a record number of lynchings across America. Blacks were strung up and hanged by overeager vigilante mobs of whites for offenses that may or may not have constituted crimes—or even taken place. Lynchings were occurring as often as three or four times per week. (By year's end, 230 known lynchings had taken place and more than two out of every three—161—were black victims.) The problem was so severe that aging black rights advocate and former abolitionist Frederick Douglass, himself a former slave, met with President Harrison at the White House to discuss the issue.

As a result of these other issues, for most of America, one black man's struggle against a single state's Jim Crow law did not seem newsworthy. Attention instead was set on the passage of even more such laws, all designed to keep the races apart and keep blacks from advancing socially and economically.

Ironically, the year marked another race-related milestone—the thirtieth anniversary of President Abraham Lincoln's drafting of the Emancipation Proclamation. In 1862, the year Lincoln issued the proclamation, Homer Plessy had been born.

During the first six months of 1892 in Louisiana, there were additional distractions and interests that might have put the *Plessy* case on the back pages of the state's newspapers. That spring, the big news item was the voting down of the relicensing of Louisiana Lottery Company's charter by the people of Louisiana. The singular political hot-button issue that had blazed through the halls of the state legislature alongside the Separate Car Law had finally been rejected. The issue had also changed the political fortunes of at least two Louisiana politicians. Senator Murphy Foster had been elected as the state's new governor, having campaigned as the anti-lottery Democratic candidate. (It had been a crowded field for governor that spring, including an anti-lottery Republican, a pro-lottery Republican, a pro-lottery Democrat, and a Populist candidate.) Foster's ascension to the governorship would also have a direct impact on the unfolding Homer Plessy court battle. One of the first appointments made by the newly seated governor was that of former Governor Nicholls, who had signed the Separate Car Act into law, to fill the chief justice seat on the Louisiana Supreme Court. Foster also appointed another jurist who would play a significant role in the *Plessy* case, as well as Desdunes's: John Ferguson as senior judge of the Orleans Parish Criminal Court. Judge Ferguson was sworn in on July 6, 1892. The *Plessy* case would unfold in Judge Ferguson's courtroom later that year.

EQUAL·JUSTICE·UNDER·LAW·

6

# Plessy and Ferguson

Martinet, Tourgée, Walker, and other interested parties prepared for the pending test case, pinning their hopes on striking down the intrastate aspect of the Separate Car Act on long-time New Orleans resident Homer Plessy. In selecting Plessy to carry their cause from an East Louisiana Railroad passenger car to the halls of Louisiana justice, the Citizens' Committee could not have made a better choice.

## AT HOME IN NEW ORLEANS

Born in March 1862, Homer Plessy was the third generation of the Plessy family to call New Orleans home. His paternal grandfather, Germain Plessy, had emigrated from France's Bordeaux region. Germain and his brother, Dominique, reached New Orleans in the early 1800s indirectly, driven north along with thousands of refugees by a successful slave uprising on the island of Sainte Dominguez (modern-day Haiti) led by the slave revolutionary Toussaint L'Ouverture. After his arrival, Germain Plessy married Catherina Mathieu, a "free woman of color" (Catherina's parents had been a white Frenchman and a free black woman). The couple produced eight children, including Homer Plessy's father, Joseph Adolphe Plessy, the seventh child, born on March 19, 1822. Joseph Plessy, called Adolphe, was baptized in the St. Louis Cathedral. (Just around the corner from the church, in the Second Recorder's Court, Homer would be brought before the bench 70 years later.)

Homer's mother, Rosa Debergue, also a "free woman of color" and of mixed blood, was born in 1835, the daughter of Michel Debergue and Josephine Blanco. Rosa worked at various common occupations, including seamstress and housekeeper. Rosa and Joseph Adolphe Plessy married, and Rosa gave birth to their first child, Ida, in November 1855. In the child's birth record, Adolphe Plessy is described as "a free man of color, a native of New Orleans, and a thirty-three-year-old carpenter."[54]

As free people of color, both Adolphe and Rosa Plessy were part of a significant group in the city's population. Prior to the Civil War, New Orleans was home to 11,000 people who fit this legal description. This group of New Orleans's residents helped build St. Augustine's Catholic Church on St. Claude Avenue. Here, the first group of black nuns, the Sisters of the Holy Family, would take their vows. The free people of color helped found other institutions of outreach in New Orleans, such as the Catholic School for Indigent Orphans. (In the 1890s, several members of the Citizens' Committee served as the school's administrators or teachers.) Many of these free black or mulatto men were hard-working middle-class artisans and professionals, such as carpenters, cigar makers, shoemakers and draymen.

Homer Plessy was a shoemaker. Women typically worked as seamstresses or ran boardinghouses.

Homer Plessy's birth certificate can still be found in the Louisiana State Archives. This document shows his birthday as March 17, 1863. At that time, the Civil War had been raging for nearly two years, and several great battles would unfold over the following months, including those at Port Hudson, Chancellorsville, and Gettysburg and the fall of Vicksburg upriver from New Orleans on the Mississippi. Federal troops had already occupied New Orleans. A month after Homer's birth, his grandfather, Germain Plessy, died. From his birth until Homer reached his teenage years, the city would remain under Union military control. Thus, young Plessy grew up in a world marked by occupation, war, martial law, emancipation, and the successes and failures of Reconstruction.

## HOMER COMES OF AGE

Just two months before Homer's sixth birthday, his father died, leaving his mother widowed and Homer an orphan. By that time, life in New Orleans had changed dramatically, with the end of the Civil War and the collapse of white political and social domination across the South:

> Indeed, Homer Plessy spent his growing years in a Louisiana where he was free to vote, engage in politics, and catch any streetcar he chose without legal molestation. In 1868, adult males, regardless of ethnicity or previous condition of slavery, could become eligible to vote by paying a $1.50 poll tax. . . . In 1869, Louisiana became the only Southern state to introduce an integrated school system, and in 1870, a Louisiana statute removed the state's ban against interracial marriages. One by one, legal barriers to public accommodations, suffrage, and education fell. In the last forty years of the nineteenth century, Louisiana's African-descent community produced an interim governor, three

lieutenant governors, six state officers, thirty-two state senators, and ninety-five state representatives.[55]

Two years after his father's death, Homer's mother remarried. Her new husband was a 36-year-old postal clerk named Victor Dupart, whose family had lived in New Orleans for several generations. Victor Dupart's family was actively engaged in politics and New Orleans society among free people of color. They "had been active in the military, in traditional occupations, in community interaction, and in politics"[56] and contributed to charities and benevolent societies and were members of Masonic societies. When he became an adult, Homer Plessy became involved in civic and social groups such as the Society of French Friends, the Cosmopolitan Mutual Aid So-

This engraving captures the scene of freedmen voting in New Orleans in 1867.

ciety, and the Scottish Rites Masons, as well as the Justice, Protective, Educational, and Social Club, through his stepfather and his family. He even served as an officer in each of these prominent organizations. Dupart had joined the Unification Movement in 1873. Possibly more than any other influence, the Dupart family had a dramatic effect on Homer Plessy's sense of civic involvement and his adult tendency toward accepting leadership.

In 1879, Homer Plessy turned 16 and was already working as a shoemaker with his stepbrother, Formidor Dupart. (Several Duparts are listed in city records as shoemakers, whereas most Plessys are shown as carpenters.) At that time, members of this trade were skilled craftsmen who fashioned shoes with a minimum of tools, using techniques that had not changed much since the Middle Ages. In the early 1890s, New Orleans was home to nearly 1,500 shoemakers; approximately one of every four was black. By 1910, there were fewer than 500 shoe craftsmen in the Crescent City. Two-thirds of them were black, and Homer Plessy was one of them.

## MAKING HIS MARK

Homer Plessy had become a prominent member of the Creole community in New Orleans by the late 1880s. Through his membership in the Justice, Protective, Educational, and Social Club, he supported advancements in education reform for the city's black children. New Orleans had been a relative model in the advancement of black civil rights and opportunities after the Civil War and during Reconstruction, but the federal occupation and control of Southern politics and social order had ended by the late 1870s. With the resultant shift back to power held by white Southerners, state funding for black schools began to dry up. Homer Plessy could remember growing up in New Orleans and attending schools where the state had provided free textbooks and the education environment was nearly free of racial prejudice and discrimination. Plessy was critical of the dwindling state support for black education—but little immediately changed for the better.

In the midst of such campaigns, Homer Plessy continued to work as a productive citizen of New Orleans, practicing his craft in a business located in the French Quarter on Dumaine Street near North Rampart. In 1888, at the age of 25, Plessy married a 19-year-old woman named Louise Bordenave. The young couple was married in St. Augustine's Church. By the following year, the Plessys were living in Faubourg Tremé, north of

 ## THE UBIQUITOUS "C"

When Homer Plessy boarded the whites-only passenger car on the East Louisiana Railroad on that fateful June day in the summer of 1892, he was barely noticed by the other passengers. He was, after all, only one-eighth black, the equivalent of having one great-grandparent who was a full-blooded black person. Plessy was so light-skinned that he was able to pass as a white person to his fellow passengers.

Many people would not consider this small level of "blood quotient" to be enough to define Plessy as a black man, but many Southern states had laws that did. Some states recognized a person as black or "colored" even if he or she was only one-sixteenth or even one-thirty-second black by ancestry. This, of course, allowed whites to define a person's race to their own satisfaction and convenience.

To keep track of who was who racially, state records often identified a person by his or her race. This was certainly the case with Homer Plessy's ancestors. Homer's paternal grandfather was a white Frenchman, Germain Plessy, and his grandmother was a "free woman of color"—Catherina Mathieu. Catherina was also the child of a white French father and a "free woman of color." Despite the intermarriages of white men and black women, the offspring born to these unions were always referred to as "colored." According to the records still kept in the Louisiana State Archives, nearly all of the Plessy family entries made prior

the French Quarter, where Creoles had lived in large numbers for the previous 80 years. Residents of this larger neighborhood were known for their "diversity, culture, politics, and music."[57] Throughout the Plessys' neighborhood, musicians performed at local clubs, halls, and dancing festivals playing traditional New Orleans Dixieland, jazz, and brass numbers. City-generated lists of the musicians living in New Orleans between 1880 and 1915 reveal that half of them lived in Creole areas, especially Faubourg Tremé.

to the Civil War were indexed with a "C" next to the person's name. The letter stood for "Colored." Similarly, Homer's mother's family, the Debergues, is found in the archives with "C" designations by their names even though Rosa Debergue's father was a white Frenchman.

This designation was intended to identify someone simply as "Colored" even if he or she was only a small fraction black by blood. Homer's father, Joseph Adolphe Plessy, is listed with a "C" by his name, even though his father and his maternal grandfather were white Frenchmen.

Other racial identifications are also found in the official records. In a childhood city record, Rosa Debergue is identified as a "free person of color," meaning that city officials listed her as black, but not a slave. In the census of 1880, Rosa is listed as "mulatto," a person of mixed white and black blood. Adolphe Plessy and Rosa Debergue were identified in the records as "free people of color," meaning that they were considered black even though Adolphe was no more than one-quarter black by ancestry.

Such records were typically confusing and did not always identify many people by their true and complete ancestry. In the minds of white record keepers, once black ancestry was included in a person's lineage, he or she would remain, as a matter of record, a black person.

Homer Plessy grew up in a New Orleans that afforded important rights to blacks, including suffrage, access to public accommodations, and education. The Abraham Lincoln School for Freedmen in New Orleans is shown above during the Reconstruction era.

## THE WORLD OF HOMER PLESSY

The part of Faubourg Tremé where the Plessys lived was one of the most pleasant in the city. They rented a recently constructed house, an elongated type domicile common in New Orleans and known as a "shotgun." ("Shotgun" houses were typically one-room wide, with rooms situated in a row behind one another, a design that would allow a person, theoretically, to fire a shotgun from the front end of the house to the back.) Nearby flowed an ancient New Orleans waterway, the Bayou St. John, whose waters reached Lake Pontchartrain. In their home located at 1108 North Claiborne, between Ursulines Street and Hospital Avenue (now known as Governor Nicholls), the Plessys were surrounded by the hustle and bustle of life in Creole New Orleans:

> Outside of Homer and Louise's front door, every four minutes, mule-powered yellow streetcars of the Canal and Claiborne line clopped by en route to open-air fruit and vegetable markets at St. Bernard Circle, about a half-mile downriver from the Plessys' house. Outside Homer and Louise's bedroom window, Congregation Hall hosted Saturday-night grand-dancing festivals where New Orleanians swayed to the sounds of Professor Joseph A. Moret's String Band. Right across Claiborne and down the Bayou Road stood the Bayou Road Boys School (colored). Plessy's walks home from Patricio Brito's shoe shop took him down the cobblestones of Ursulines Street, past a lumberyard, stables, corner grocery stores with second-story residences, and Economy Hall, where Louis Armstrong would later trumpet New Orleans music with crafted abandon. In Tremé, townhouses with wrought-iron second-story balconies, and villas with stately center halls, stood next to petite plastered-brick Creole cottages and former slave quarters that were converted into backyard apartments.[58]

In Homer and Louise Plessy's neighborhood (Homer was registered to vote in the Sixth Ward's Third Precinct) were people of many races, ethnicities, and national origins. It was a polyglot (multilingual) mix of blacks and whites and those in between. Scots lived in close proximity with Mexicans; West Indians walked the same streets as Germans. It was a world as varied as the jobs the people held and the professions they represented, including doctors, barbers, grocers, carpenters, cigar makers, bakers, and barrel makers.

The Plessys' neighborhood was not a perfect world, of course. There was a prison close by, as well as a red-light district called Storyville. The year before Plessy boarded the "wrong" car of the East Louisiana Railroad, 11 Italian immigrants had been killed—gunned down and lynched. Homer Plessy had made his home there, however, and he had become an involved, caring professional, a citizen of New Orleans who wanted his world and that of his neighbors to be as good as it could be. With state-supported—even mandated—segregation increasingly the law of the land, he was compelled to fight against a trend that he considered a step back into a racist past.

## THE LIFE OF JOHN HOWARD FERGUSON

When the *Plessy* case came before him in November 1892, Judge John Ferguson had been presiding over his court for only four months. The role he would play in the *Plessy* case would prove

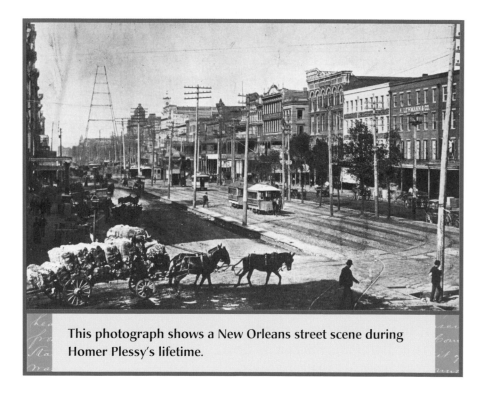

This photograph shows a New Orleans street scene during Homer Plessy's lifetime.

crucial, however. He came to the court not as a lifelong resident of New Orleans, or even of Louisiana, but as a New Englander, the product of a region that had led the cause of abolition and antislavery sentiment before the Civil War. He would not be the only judge from New England and Massachusetts to hear the *Plessy* case: When the case reached the United States Supreme Court, half of the eight justices had at one time or another called Massachusetts home.

John Ferguson was old enough to be Homer Plessy's father. He was born on Martha's Vineyard in 1838. At that time, the island was known for its fishing industry. Great masted ships, including "fleets of whaling ships that charged headlong into icy, rough Atlantic seas scouring the area for whales,"[59] sailed past Martha's Vineyard daily. A lifetime as a shipmaster was often quite lucrative, and shipmasters were a widely respected breed of men. In retirement, they typically became the leading citizens of the small seaports where they lived. One of the island's native sea captains was John Ferguson's father. Today, the streets and landmarks of Martha's Vineyard often are named after these titans of the sea.

Surrounded by the sea and raised with a Puritan ethic, young Ferguson left home to study law in Boston after his twenty-first birthday. Ferguson the law student lived in a boarding house on Summer Street, just a few blocks from the law offices of Benjamin Franklin Hallett, Ferguson's law instructor. (Boston's City Hall was located next door to Hallett's law practice.) All around him, Ferguson saw the vestiges of Boston's role in the American Revolution. He walked past the Old South Meeting House on his way to law classes. It was here that Samuel Adams had called for Parliament to repeal the tax on tea in 1773, followed that same day by the Boston Tea Party. The black poet Phillis Wheatley had worshiped in the Congregational meeting house. Near Ferguson's lodgings was the Granary Burial Ground, where the remains of Paul Revere, Samuel Adams, and Crispus Attucks, a freed black who was killed in 1770 during the Boston

Massacre, were buried. Just up the street from where he studied law, Ferguson could see Faneuil Hall, where America's most famous leaders, including George Washington and abolitionist leaders Frederick Douglass and William Lloyd Garrison, had gathered and spoken. Hallett had also delivered speeches in that hall.

Studying law under Benjamin Hallett was an exciting experience for young John Ferguson. Hallett was known as a leader in the Democratic Party. In his late 60s, Hallett was known not only as a skilled lawyer but also as an abolitionist, politician, and temperance reformer. Hallett was resolute in his opposition to slavery. He had helped frame the position of many Northern Democrats regarding the institution: "We are opposed to slavery in every form and color, and in favor of freedom and free soil wherever man lives throughout God's heritage."[60] He had served as an editor and journalist for various political publications and was a regular speaker at Democratic Party conventions. He had argued cases before the United States Supreme Court. Hallett would side with the Union during the Civil War, but he died in 1862.

At the time of Hallett's death, John Ferguson had recently completed his law studies and, by the following year, was in practice for himself. His first law office was in the shadow of Hallett's old offices, at 20 Court Street. When the war ended in 1865, the city of New Orleans was occupied by Union forces that included two regiments of Massachusetts soldiers. Two of the generals who governed over the city while it was under martial law were from Massachusetts—Benjamin Butler and Nathaniel Banks. Ferguson became interested in New Orleans after hearing from returning Massachusetts troops of the opportunities available to Northerners in the defeated South. By then in his late 20s, the world seemed open to lawyer John Ferguson. He decided to leave for the Crescent City.

EQUAL·JUSTICE·UNDER·LAW·

# 7

# Plessy Meets Ferguson

N ew Orleans was still under federal control when Ferguson arrived and would remain so until 1877. Northerners were flocking to the city, all seeking to "take possession of commerce and politics, to whatever extent it was possible."[61] By 1866, Ferguson had established a law practice in the city, setting up shop in the Morris Building in the uptown commercial district of New Orleans. That same year, Ferguson courted and married Virginia Earhart, the daughter of a prominent native New Orleans lawyer who had denounced slavery before the war and did not support the Confederacy during the war.

## FERGUSON IN NEW ORLEANS

In time, John and Virginia Ferguson moved outside the city to the small upriver community of Burtheville. They raised three children and enjoyed suburban life in a cottage home Ferguson helped build. (Judge Ferguson's home still stands at 1500 Henry Clay.) The Ferguson family attended the local St. Charles Avenue Christian Church. Just as Homer Plessy was a socially involved civic leader, so was Ferguson. He joined the Knights of Pythias, a charitable organization founded by Congress in 1864, its purpose being "for the reuniting of our brethren in the North and the South, for teaching the people to love one another."[62]

Ferguson had immigrated to New Orleans from Massachusetts in search of opportunity, and those opportunities came to him with regularity. After starting a successful law practice, he was catapulted into the arena of Southern Democrat politics in 1877 with the end of Northern-controlled Reconstruction in Louisiana. That year, Francis T. Nicholls, who had served as a Confederate general during the Civil War, became the state's new governor. Although Nicholls would prove to be no ally or supporter of blacks and Creoles in Louisiana, his ascendance presented another opportunity to John Ferguson. As Nicholls personally redrew the membership in the state's legislature, he selected Ferguson to assume the seat of a black representative, Aristide Dejoie. Ferguson became the representative of New Orleans's uptown district on March 5, 1877. He was 39 years old. Ferguson did not remain a legislator for long, however: He was voted out in 1878 with the reelection of Dejoie.

Ferguson continued to practice law through the next decade. He spent years practicing civil law, but by 1891, he turned to criminal law. That year, he agreed to serve as one of two defense attorneys for Charles Paterno, an Italian immigrant to New Orleans who was accused of killing David Hennessy, the city's chief of police. (The case never went to trial.) The following year would prove a watershed in Ferguson's long legal

PEOPLES SERIES.

AMERICAN VIEWS

St. Patrick's Hall in New Orleans, where Homer Plessy was tried for violating the Separate Car Act, is shown in this late nineteenth century stereoscopic slide.

career. By then, Ferguson had been practicing law in Louisiana for a quarter century. Having become a prominent figure in the city, he actively campaigned on behalf of several Democratic candidates. He spoke to crowds in 20 Louisiana parishes in support of State Senator Murphy Foster's campaign for governor. He also spoke out against the Louisiana Lottery Company. For his active endorsement and support, Ferguson was rewarded by Foster, who had won the governorship, with the vacant judgeship in Orleans Parish Section A. (Judge Robert Marr had disappeared on the day of the election in May.)

Judge Ferguson was sworn in on July 5, 1892, and soon took his place on the bench in the Criminal Courts Building, located at the corner of Lafayette and Camp streets. (At that time, the building was popularly known as St. Patrick's Hall.) The courthouse was in the heart of the busy world of New Orleans's city government. Nearby, at Lafayette Square, were government and legal offices. Across the street from the Criminal Courts Building stood Gallier Hall, the center of New Orleans's government.

Close at hand was the First District Court building and a precinct police station. In taking his judgeship, Ferguson was accepting his role as senior criminal court judge and would serve
the four remaining years of Judge Marr's term.

## PLESSY APPEARS BEFORE FERGUSON

On October 11, 1892, Homer Plessy received notification that he
was to appear before Judge Ferguson. His case would be number 19117. He was charged with violating the Separate Car Act,
which is exactly the charge for which the Citizens' Committee
had hoped. The case had originally been set for hearing months
earlier, but Ferguson had postponed the hearing for cases he
considered more important. During the months between its
original date and the October hearing, Judge Ferguson's court
had heard cases concerning embezzlement, aggravated assault,
larceny, and a stabbing. There had been concealed weapons cases, as well as one that involved horse stealing. A case involving a
violation of the state's Separate Car Law was considered minor,
indeed.

Two days later, on October 13, all the important players,
including Homer Plessy; his attorney, James Walker, whose offices were only two blocks from the court building; Louis Martinet and Rodolphe Desdunes; and the prosecuting attorney,
Lionel Adams, appeared before Judge Ferguson in the Criminal Courts Building. It was a pleasant fall day in New Orleans,
with a scattering of showers and a slightly cool temperature for
the Crescent City, about 70 degrees. As Judge Ferguson entered
the courtroom, he was prepared to hear the case, one seemingly
open and shut—*The State of Louisiana v. Homer Adolph Plessy*.

The attorney representing the state was a skilled prosecutor.
Lionel Adams had begun serving as the city's district attorney in
1884. Only recently, he had accepted the role of assistant district
attorney temporarily to allow another city attorney, Charles
Butler, the opportunity to experience the rigors of the city's top
legal position. Adams was thus a seasoned criminal attorney,

one who not only served as prosecutor but also as defense attorney from time to time. In 1891, he had defended the Italian immigrants who were charged with the murder of New Orleans's police chief, David Hennessy.

Adams had a formidable opponent in defense counsel Walker. Now a man in his mid-50s, Walker had served in the Confederate Army during the Civil War and was mustered out as a private. He had joined the Republican Party during Reconstruction. Over the years, however, Walker had abandoned politics. As described by Martinet, Walker was a "good, upright, and conscientious man."[63] Walker had not taken the *Plessy* case *pro bono* (without a fee), but he had agreed to only take $1,000, less than half as much as another lawyer Martinet had considered hiring. At Walker's side in the courtroom that day was Homer Plessy.

As the case opened, attorney Walker called for a dismissal of the charges against Plessy, saying that the Separate Car Law was unconstitutional. He then proceeded to present Homer Plessy to Judge Ferguson as an upstanding citizen, one who had boarded the East Louisiana Railroad passenger car with the appropriate ticket, had remained well-mannered during his confrontation with the train's conductor, and was a man of principle. Walker also criticized the law for putting too much responsibility on the conductor, as the Separate Car Act granted him "the power to determine the question of race and to assort the passengers on his train."[64] He also presented the obvious to the judge: that Homer Plessy had no more appearance of being a black man than Judge Ferguson did. The law made an issue of race, and "the state has no power to authorize any person to determine the [race of a person] without testimony, or to make the rights and privileges of any citizen of the United States dependent on the fact of race."[65] Walker concluded his presentation by filing a motion to postpone the trial so that arguments could be made concerning the constitutionality of the Separate Car Law. If the act was concluded to be unconstitutional, then there was no case against Plessy. Judge Ferguson accepted Walker's motion and set a date for another appearance for Plessy before his court two weeks later—October 28.

When the day arrived, Plessy had his second day in court. Just as he had earlier in Ferguson's court, Walker hammered at his main points concerning the unconstitutionality of the Separate Car Law. In making his presentation before the court, prosecutor Adams argued that the state had a perfect right to establish laws according to its own views and values regarding any interaction between the races. The day ended with Judge Ferguson adjourning the case, stating that he would begin to consider his decision in his chambers. Before he left the courtroom, Ferguson complimented Walker on his presentation of the case and his keen understanding of the issues surrounding the Separate Car Law.

Three weeks passed before Judge Ferguson reconvened his court and rendered his decision for or against Plessy. The time had been extended in part due to an extensive strike that hit New Orleans when perhaps as many as 25,000 black and white union workers walked off their jobs. Only Governor Foster's threat to send the state militia to break up the general strike brought an end to the wide-scale labor stoppage. Once the strike was over, Judge Ferguson announced his decision in favor of the law on November 18. In his ruling, he stated of Plessy's challenge that the law provided equal accommodations for passengers such as Plessy. That being the case, Plessy had only been denied the privilege of asserting his personal will and violating the law. In addition, Ferguson argued that a state had the right and power to regulate railroads operating strictly within the borders of that state. Plessy, Martinet, and the Citizens' Committee had lost their day in court. The Citizens' Committee had never intended this court's decision to represent the final word on the case, however. Walker wasted little time in appealing the Louisiana Supreme Court to overturn Judge Ferguson's decision.

THE STATE OF LOUISIANA, | PARISH OF ORLEANS.
ss.
Criminal District Court for the Parish of Orleans.

LIONEL ADAMS, District Attorney for the Parish of Orleans, who, in the name and by the authority of the said State, prosecutes in this behalf, in proper person comes into the Criminal District Court for the Parish of Orleans, in the Parish of Orleans, and gives the said Court here to understand and be informed, that one *Homer Adolph Plessy*

late of the Parish of Orleans, on the *Seventh* day of *June* in the year of our Lord one thousand eight hundred and *ninety two*, with force and arms in the Parish of Orleans aforesaid, and within the jurisdiction of the Criminal District Court for the Parish of Orleans *being then a passenger traveling wholly within the limits of the State of Louisiana, on a passenger train belonging to the East Louisiana Railroad Company, a railway company carrying passengers in their Coaches within the State of Louisiana, and which the Officers of the said East Louisiana Railroad Company had power and were required to assign, and did assign the said Homer Adolph Plessy to the coach used for the race to which he, the said Homer Adolph Plessy belonged — unlawfully did then and there insist on going into a Coach to which by race he did not belong*

contrary to the form of the Statute of the State of Louisiana in such case made and provided, and against the peace and dignity of the same. *(Signed) Lionel Adams*
District Attorney for the Parish of Orleans.

This court document, dated June 7, 1892, states Homer Plessy's crime as "unlawfully… insist[ing] on going into a Coach to which by race he did not belong."

## BEFORE THE LOUISIANA HIGH COURT

As attorneys Tourgée and Walker prepared to present their case before the Louisiana Supreme Court, they were fully aware that the state's highest court decided cases on "common law, statutes, and interpretations of the federal constitution."[66] The lawyers would rest their case on their interpretations of two amendments to the U.S. Constitution, both of which had been passed and ratified during the days of Reconstruction: the thirteenth and the fourteenth.

The Thirteenth Amendment had provided for the abolition of slavery and involuntary servitude, and the Fourteenth established citizenship, both state and federal, to "all persons born or naturalized in the United States." In addition, this amendment guaranteed "the privileges or immunities of citizens," "equal protection of the laws," and freedom or protection from being deprived, by either the state or the federal government, "of life, liberty, or property, without due process of law."

## ALBION TOURGÉE: POPULAR NOVELIST

Although Albion Tourgée would leave his mark on the pages of American history as the primary counsel who guided the *Plessy* case through the nation's legal system, he was known during his lifetime for more than his legal expertise. More than 20 years before the *Plessy* case was heard by the U.S. Supreme Court, Tourgée had begun his other career—as a popular novelist.

His first novel was written in 1874 under the title *Toinette, a Novel*. The book was published under the pen name Henry Churton. Tourgée set the novel with fictional characters and places, but his intent was to use his fiction writing as an avenue for expressing his feelings on various social and political topics. It was an approach to his writing that Tourgée took quite seriously. "A novel without a purpose is the counterpart of a man without a purpose," Tourgée once wrote. "One written for mere amusement may be either good or bad, but at the very best, is only the lowest form of art."*

Other novels followed, including *Figs and Thistles* and, perhaps his best work, *A Fool's Errand*. Of all his novels, *A Fool's Errand* was the most autobiographical. The novel was set in the South (Tourgée had then been living in North Carolina) during Reconstruction. He wrote the book to present how Southerners' minds had been changed for the better by the years of federal occupation and social alteration. Tourgée's goal in writing *A Fool's Errand* was to "build a bridge from Negro emancipation to Negro equality."**

Tourgée and Walker framed their arguments in light of the guarantees granted by these amendments. Just as the Thirteenth Amendment had abolished slavery, it had also, they would argue, render later attempts to limit the rights of blacks illegal. In the legal minds of these two attorneys, the Thirteenth Amendment

The "fools" referred to in the book's title were "those idealists who believed in liberty and equality despite the negativity and protestations of others who thought that people of different classes, races, or regions were incapable of unity or racial progress."*** President James Garfield lauded the novel, expressing his personal desire that the United States be a "paradise for all such fools."† He also summoned Tourgée to the White House after taking office in 1881. He told the Southern writer and attorney, "But for the publication of your work, I do not think my election would have been possible."†† The novel proved extremely popular with Northern readers and its publication, as well as that of his next novel, *Bricks Without Straw*, were both financial successes. Tourgée also wrote important essays and nonfiction works, including one on the topic of the Ku Klux Klan. There were other, later novels, including *The Man Who Outlived Himself*, as well as books of nonfiction, but they were not as commercially successful. By the 1880s, his fiction writing had made him wealthy and well-known across America. This level of financial security and public fame allowed him to take on the *Plessy* case without pay, helping further his literary intent of creating a man of purpose as well as a novel of purpose.

*Quoted in Medley, *We as Freedmen*, p. 59.
**Ibid.
***Ibid.
†Ibid.
††Ibid.

also outlawed racial discrimination that was designed to mark blacks with any "badge of servitude."[67] This argument would render all Jim Crow laws and Black Codes illegal as violations of the Thirteenth Amendment. The attorneys could cite examples of steps Congress had taken after the passage of the Thirteenth Amendment to strike down laws that restricted black freedoms, including the Civil Rights Act of 1866, "which was drafted to override the Black Codes, to offer an inclusive definition of citizenship, and to safeguard the freedmen's civil rights."[68]

The Thirteenth Amendment was important to Tourgée and Walker in forming their approach to presenting before the state Supreme Court, but the Fourteenth Amendment was the linchpin, the center of Plessy's case. The Thirteenth Amendment had abolished slavery, thus allowing citizenship for blacks (black citizenship had been denied by an earlier U.S. Supreme Court decision, *Dred Scott v. Sandford,* decided in 1857), but the Fourteenth Amendment was created to destroy the significance and relevance of the *Dred Scott* decision and provided blacks with a lengthy list of rights and privileges under federal law. Presented to the states for ratification just months after Congress's passage of the Civil Rights Act of 1866, the Fourteenth Amendment in many ways represented a bill of rights for blacks and other minorities, protecting from infringement by the states. Congress was angered by the creation of Black Codes in many Southern states; each code was designed to cut into the rights of blacks. At that time, Congress made the ratification of the Fourteenth Amendment a prerequisite for the readmission of any former Confederate state into the Union. The amendment was ratified in 1868.

## "PRIVILEGES" AND "IMMUNITIES"

In presenting their case in November 1892, Tourgée and Walker wanted to convince the Louisiana justices that the Separate Car Law had violated Plessy's "privileges" and "immunities" when he was removed from the first-class car on the East Louisiana line.

Because the intent of the law was based in prejudice, how could the Separate Car Law be considered constitutional? To Plessy's attorneys, the purpose of the law was clear and unmistakable:

> Although the law's stated purpose was promoting "the comfort of passengers on railway trains," they wanted to know, wasn't its net effect to make racist whites feel better but excluded blacks feel inferior? Passengers, no matter what their race, were supposedly equal in being transported to the same destinations, but it must have been obvious to everyone that accommodations for blacks in the Jim Crow cars were far poorer than those for white passengers.[69]

Plessy's lawyers were also concerned about a questionable phrasing in the Separate Car Law. The act used the term "persons of the colored race." To whom, they asked, did this specifically refer and apply? Some people could obviously be taken for black, but this was not the case with Plessy. He and others like him, those "in whom color is not discernible,"[70] could be assigned to a whites-only or colored car according to the view of the conductor on a specific railcar.

The challenge of the Separate Car Law was that the issue of who is black and who is white could not be answered definitively:

> Light-skinned Negroes would not be able to tell how they were supposed to fit into the law's black-and-white categories, and if they guessed wrong they could find themselves, at the least, deprived of the value of the first-class ticket they purchased or, at worst, arrested for remaining in a "whites only" seat in defiance of the conductor's order. In either case they would have sacrificed their self-respect or their money and, thus, would have been deprived of their property (or its equivalent) without "due process of law."[71]

Equally to the point was the practice of allowing some exceptions to the law. For example, a black nurse would be allowed to sit on a whites-only car alongside her white patient.

Black nannies charged with seeing after a white or mixed child could sit in the whites-only car along with their white employers. In the case of a racially mixed family, however, a white husband could be separated from his black wife and their children, who would have to sit in the "black car." According to Tourgée and Walker, this violated a husband's "absolute right to the companionship and society of his wife" by separating them from one another based on race during their train ride. As they worded their brief, "Thus the bottom rail is on the top; the nurse is admitted to a privilege which the wife herself does not enjoy."[72]

Tourgée and Walker also included mention of the dualistic nature of the Separate Car Law. The law sought to segregate blacks from whites on passenger trains, which were large and spacious and often did not place the races into close proximity to one another, but it exempted streetcars. These cars were

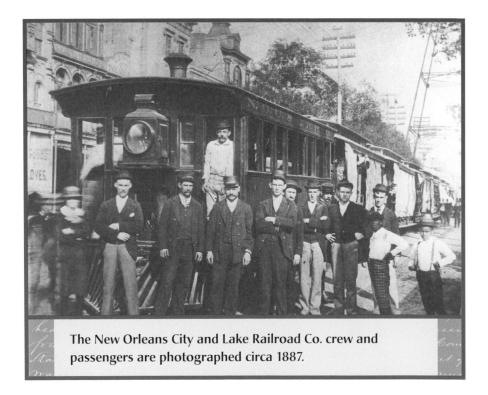

The New Orleans City and Lake Railroad Co. crew and passengers are photographed circa 1887.

much smaller than railroad cars, and passengers riding them often found themselves elbow to elbow with all races. The brief argued that the contact between the races on streetcars was closer and more frequent than on rail passenger cars. Streetcars in New Orleans, of course, had been segregated 25 years earlier, only to be protested by the city's black and Creole population, which led to their integration. The Tourgée-Walker brief made no mention of this historic precedent.

In the end, the Tourgée-Walker brief asserted the clear contention that the men who had created the Separate Car Law had done so not to create a truly separate but equal world designed to allow for "the comfort of passengers on railway trains," but to "legalize a discrimination between classes of citizens based on color."[73]

When Walker presented his case to the high court's justices on November 22, 1892, the Louisiana Supreme Court upheld Judge Ferguson's decision. It did not accept Walker's claim that the Separate Car Law was a violation of the Thirteenth or Fourteenth Amendment. The decision by the Louisiana high court did not come as a surprise to the Citizens' Committee or to Plessy. After all, the court's chief justice was newly appointed Francis Nicholls, the former Louisiana governor who had signed the Separate Car Law into legal existence. The Louisiana trials were simply the hurdles the Citizens' Committee had known that they would have to jump to get their case to the court that would ultimately settle the issue of "separate but equal" segregation—the United States Supreme Court.

EQUAL·JUSTICE·UNDER·LAW·

# 8

# Before the Supreme Court

L ess than two months after the ruling by the Louisiana Supreme Court, Tourgée and Walker filed for the *Plessy* case to be heard by the United States Supreme Court. Tourgée, Walker, Martinet, and the Citizens' Committee were intent on getting the case before the highest court in the land as quickly as possible. If the attorneys for Plessy had continued to push for the case to be presented before the nine justices of the Supreme Court, the case likely would have been heard by the fall of 1893 or early 1894 at the latest. That spring, however, Homer Plessy's case seemed to face an unlikely future. Tourgée appears to have expressed the first concern that the political and social

climate in the country was not favorable to the advancement
of his client's case and the cause of the Citizens' Committee. In
addition, he did not believe that there were enough justices on
the high court who would decide in favor of Plessy. As Tourgée
viewed the court's membership that spring, he "estimated that
only one Justice would firmly lean to Plessy's side, three would
be uncertain and five, frankly opposed."[74]

## DELAYING THE CASE

As Tourgée studied the possibilities of an audience before this
group of justices on the Supreme Court, he became convinced
that he and Walker would lose if they argued their case in 1893.
In addition to the court's unsympathetic membership, events
taking place across the United States revealed a dark atmo-
sphere concerning the security and advancement of the nation's
blacks. Lynchings were taking place with increasing regularity in
1893—a total of 118 blacks were lynched that year, and one out
of every three lynchings took place in Louisiana. Hate groups
across the country seemed to be calling loudly for reductions
in black freedom. The Ku Klux Klan was mounting a harsh
campaign of violence against blacks across the South. In 1892,
there was so much racism in America that Grover Cleveland,
the Democratic candidate for president, "won the White House
partly by tarring Republicans with their attempts to guarantee
civil rights to African Americans."[76] An editorial featured in *The
Christian Recorder* in 1892 was plainspoken in the truth of the
matter: "It is evident that the white people of the South have no
further use for the Negro. He is being treated worse now than at
any other time since the surrender [of the South at the end of
the Civil War in 1865]."[77]

In 1894, the trend against blacks continued. Specifically, in
Louisiana, the legislature enacted new laws restricting interracial marriage and segregating blacks and whites into separate
waiting rooms in railroad depots and stations across the state.

The climate of segregation was even given a boost by Booker T. Washington, one of the recognized black leaders of the day. In September 1895, while attending the Atlanta Exposition, a world's fair, Washington delivered a speech in which he appeared to sanction the concept and practice of segregation. In his words:

> In all things that are purely social, we can be as separate as the fingers, yet one as the hand in all things essential to mutual progress. . . . The wisest among my race understand that the agitation of questions of social equality is the extremest folly, and that progress in the enjoyment of all the privileges that will come to us must be the result of severe and constant struggle rather than of artificial forcing.[78]

Washington was simply arguing that "in the face of white hatred, integration simply stirred up opposition."[79]

In an environment where segregation had found acceptance even in the mind of a national black leader, supporters of the *Plessy* case became concerned that they might fail in their efforts. Martinet expressed his concerns to Tourgée as early as 1893:

> The question forces itself upon me, are we not fighting a hopeless battle—a battle made doubly hopeless by the tyranny and cruelty of the Southern white? Are the Negroes progressing, or are they not retrograding under the yoke of the Southern barbarians? . . . The Booker Washingtons . . . & others have their uses & are doing a useful work. . . . But if our fight is fruitless, or rather our own manner of fighting . . . so what is to be done?[80]

Despite such misgivings, the Citizens' Committee eventually decided to take the Plessy case forward. A few weeks after Washington's speech at the Atlanta Exposition, everything appeared ready for presentation to the Supreme Court. By late fall, Albion Tourgée had filed the appropriate and final papers for a hearing during the October 1895 term of the high court. As Tourgée readied himself for the coming showdown before the Supreme Court, he knew he would have an uphill battle. They had waited nearly three years for the membership of the court to turn in favor of Plessy's cause, but now the court was probably even less sympathetic than ever. Since 1892, two new justices had come on the court. Edward D. White was from Louisiana and had once served in the Confederate Army. A New Yorker, Rufus Peckham, was also new to the court and was considered one of its most conservative members. The Court's chief justice was 66-year-old Melville W. Fuller, who had been appointed to lead the court in 1888 by President Cleveland. Fuller was considered an "old time Democrat, friendly to the doctrine of state rights, and as a sincere believer in individualism."[81]

Tourgée had received word from the Court's clerk that the *Plessy* case would appear before the justices on April 13, the second Monday of the month. Tourgée was informed of this only days before. The short notice would not allow Martinet enough time to travel from Louisiana to Washington to witness the proceedings. Walker was ill and had to excuse himself. That Friday, April 10, Tourgée boarded a train near his home in Mayfield, New York, bound for Washington. He would be assisted in the courtroom by another attorney, an old friend, Samuel F. Phillips. Phillips was an expert on property rights. The state of Louisiana would be represented by Alexander Porter Morse, a Louisiana native who lived in Washington and whose specialty was presenting federal appeals cases.

## COURT IN SESSION

The membership of the United States Supreme Court had changed significantly during the ten years leading up to 1896, the year the *Plessy* case finally got its hearing. During that decade, seven justices had gone off the court, only to be replaced by new justices who did not believe that Reconstruction had been a success. They did not fully support the concept of the federal government intervening on behalf of the nation's black population or support the idea that the government's job was to protect and guarantee their rights. They tended to believe that "blacks must fend for themselves."[75] Two of the justices had been on the court during Reconstruction: John Marshall Harlan from Kentucky, who had been appointed by President Hayes, and Stephen J. Field, the court's oldest member. He had been named to the Supreme Court in 1863 by President Lincoln.

In 1896, the Supreme Court held its sessions in a smallish courtroom in the U.S. Capitol building. The room had been used previously as the Senate Chamber. The members of the court sat along a lengthy table flanked by a row of marble columns. There were benches with red velvet cushions for spectators. Tourgée took his seat on one of these cushions. At noon, eight justices, robed in black, filed in, led by the marshal of the Court. The ninth justice, David J. Brewer, had recused himself from the proceedings. He never gave an explanation.

The interior of a Supreme Court room in the U.S. Capitol.

At the time the *Plessy* case was presented to the Supreme Court, oral arguments were not recorded verbatim (they would not be until the 1950s), so Tourgée's exact words to the eight justices are not known. Tourgée, did, however, make a transcription of his 44-page presentation to the court afterward; today this document is included in his papers at the Chautauqua County Historical Society in Westfield, New York. With only 30 minutes to present his case to the court, he managed to include as many legal arguments as he could. He naturally argued, as he had before to the Louisiana Supreme Court, that the matter before the court was a federal issue, one that should not remain in the hands of the states. He emphasized the citizenship of blacks in America, which had been guaranteed to them by the passage of the Reconstruction Amendments—the Thirteenth, Fourteenth, and Fifteenth—laws that clearly left the definition of citizenship in the hands of the federal government, not the states. In his words:

> The old citizenship of the United States was determined by race or descent. The new citizenship of the United States had nothing to do with race or descent. Under the pre-existing law no man having a drop of colored blood in his veins, could become a citizen of the United States. It was in all literalness a "white man's government." In the new citizenship color is expressly ignored and the sole condition of citizenship, is birth in the United States.[82]

As to the Separate Car Act, which was the focal point of the case, Tourgée reminded the justices that the law placed a tremendous burden on the railroads and was just one more means of regulating big business. He hoped that this argument would ring true to many of the Supreme Court justices who, as a matter of record, were opposed to regulatory laws placed on businesses by the government. To this matter, he argued that the Separate Car Law was ridiculous in its premise. The law represented a regulatory restriction based solely on race. "What is the purpose

of the act?" he asked the justices. "Evidently to assort passengers
. . . according to color."[83] Tourgée then made an issue of the term
"colored race." Although it was generally understood that the
Louisiana Separate Car Law was designed to keep the black and
white races from sharing railroad cars, the act simply divided
all people into two races: white and the "colored race." Tourgée
argued that the category "colored race" was too vague, even un-
scientific. Surely science recognizes a variety of different races,
Tourgée stated, including Mongolians and Indians. Technically,
then, those who created the Separate Car statute managed to
"reduce the whole human family to two grand divisions which
they term 'races'. . . . It is a new ethnology but prejudice based on
the lessons of slavery."[84]

In his conclusion to the Court, Tourgée summed up by
making a bold statement that he took for fact: that the Separate

 **THE ROOM WHERE
THE LAW WAS DECIDED**

When the justices gathered to hear the *Plessy v. Ferguson* case,
the United States Supreme Court was meeting in the old Senate
chamber. The Senate had abandoned the chamber after the addition of two new wings to the Capitol building just before the
Civil War. The Court's former chamber, a dark basement room
where the *Dred Scott* case had been heard in 1857, had been
turned into a law library. There were few additional official spac-
es provided for the members of the Supreme Court at that time.
Instead, they used a conference room in the Capitol basement,
next to the law library, where they could meet informally in small
groups and discuss legal matters. Otherwise, when writing their
legal opinions, they did so in private offices or in their studies
at home.

Car Act had no purpose but to keep blacks out of railroad cars used by whites solely to make whites more comfortable, "not to keep whites out of another car for the comfort and satisfaction of the colored passenger."[85] By doing so, the law was a blatant "attempt to evade the constitutional requirements of equality of right and legal privilege to all citizens and to avoid the decisions of this court in regard to legislation intended to discriminate against the colored citizen by professing to discriminate against both."[86] In Tourgée's words, "A race or class claiming superiority . . . desires to see its exclusiveness crystallized into law. . . . The claim that this act is for the common advantage of both races . . . is farcical."[87] The result was "to perpetuate the stigma of color—to make the curse immortal, incurable, inevitable."[88]

## SPEAKING FOR THE STATE

After Tourgée's presentation before the Court, Alexander Morse presented his arguments on behalf of Judge Ferguson and the state of Louisiana. Basically, Tourgée's case was met by four primary points. Morse argued that it was perfectly within the scope of state power for its legislature to enact laws "to promote the comfort of passengers on railway trains."[89] As such, the Separate Car Law represented only an effort by the state to regulate, on behalf of the people of Louisiana, how passenger trains operated within its borders. The law, the state's attorney claimed, was "designed to prevent problems that could prove harmful to society if such regulation were left entirely to the whims and passions of each passenger riding the train."[90] Morse's second point made the claim that the Separate Car Law did not deprive any passenger of his or her claim to equal rights and their protection under the law. Instead, Morse claimed, the railroads were, under the car law, expected to provide equal accommodations for black and white passengers. This was a point that had been accepted by the Louisiana Supreme Court. The law was legal in that it provided accommodations to both races equally. In fact, there had been no evidence presented at the state level that the railroads had not provided for both races.

Morse's third argument was that such laws were common practice, not only across the South, but in the Northern states

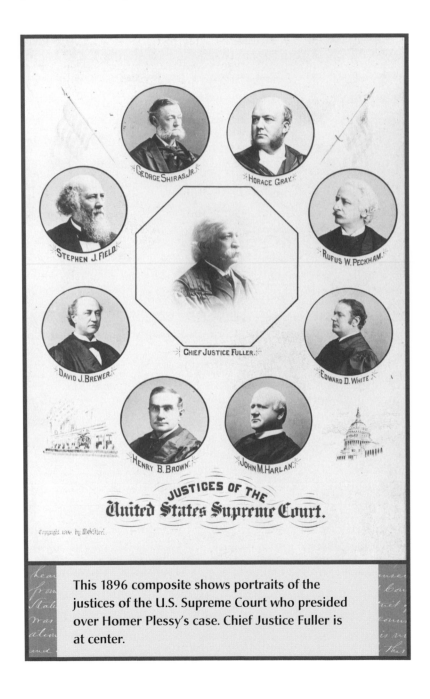

This 1896 composite shows portraits of the justices of the U.S. Supreme Court who presided over Homer Plessy's case. Chief Justice Fuller is at center.

as well. Segregation was a way of life in the North, stated Morse, who gave examples including schools, churches, and even the military. (He made the point that, during the Civil War, the North had fought to eliminate slavery while keeping its military units segregated. At the time of the *Plessy* case, the U.S. military was still segregated.) Interracial marriages were typically illegal in both the North and South. Segregation, said Morse, was simply part of the social fabric of American life and the nation's laws, including those of the states, were designed to reflect that reality.

Last, the case against Plessy was furthered by the claim that it was constitutional for the states to exert their power, that the federal government should be restrained from interfering with the rightful and legitimate expression of power wielded by the states. The Separate Car Law was just such an expression. Because the Louisiana law promised to require railroads to provide "separate but equal" accommodations, the rights of Homer Plessy and all nonwhites who were restricted from using whites-only railcars had not been violated.

Once Morse completed his arguments on behalf of the state of Louisiana, Plessy's other attorney, S.F. Phillips, presented further arguments. According to his brief, Phillips "claimed that a state's power to exercise its regulatory police powers differed when applied to railroad cars and to schools."[91] This was an important argument, since schools in Washington, DC, were segregated and the same Congress that had passed the Thirteenth and Fourteenth Amendments allowed those schools to exist. (Under the U.S. Constitution, Congress has the authority to administer the laws for the District of Columbia.) Phillips argued that schools as institutions of learning were actually extensions of other institutions, such as marriage and the family. With the future of each generation dependent on these institutions, states had the right to pass appropriate laws defining these institutions. Phillips argued that "the fate of future generations in no way depended on seating in railroad cars."[92] Thus, any state attempt to place the existence of segregated schools on the same legal plane as the Separate Car Law was not applicable.

With these arguments made, the case of *Plessy v. Ferguson* now lay in the hands of the United States Supreme Court—in the hands of eight white men, ages 51 to 80. After the presentation of the case, Tourgée remained in Washington for a few more days and then left for his home in Mayville on April 16. He would have to wait more than a month before the justices handed down their decision.

9

# Deciding for the Future

On May 18, 1896, the justices on the Supreme Court announced their decision. Nearly four years had passed since Homer Plessy had boarded a whites-only passenger car on the East Louisiana Railroad. With a count of seven to one, the majority of the court decided against Homer Plessy and in favor of the Separate Car Law, as well as other similar laws. The decision appeared to legitimize Jim Crow laws across the country.

## THE MAJORITY SPEAKS

The majority decision of the Supreme Court was written by Justice Henry Billings Brown, a Northerner and the son of a wealthy Massachusetts businessman. As a young attorney, he had specialized in admiralty law. As a jurist, Brown was a protective advocate of business and property rights. Through his Republican connections, he had served on various courts, including the U.S. District Court in eastern Michigan. In 1890, he had been tapped for the Supreme Court by Republican President Benjamin Harrison. In writing for the court's majority, Brown stated that the Fourteenth Amendment's "equal protection" clause applied only to state laws that discriminated against blacks as a class of people. On the surface, this application to the Separate Car Law would indicate that the law was unconstitutional and that Plessy had a justifiable reason to defy the law. The court skirted that by redefining exactly *what privileges* were protected by the Fourteenth Amendment. The wording of the amendment referred to the "privileges" and "immunities" of citizenship in the United States. In upholding the Louisiana Separate Car Law, the Supreme Court decided that states had the latitude and legal freedom to define what constitutes a proper privilege in that state relative to citizenship in that state. Using this dualistic definition of privileges and immunities of citizenship, the Court was stating that the Fourteenth Amendment did not represent a conflict with the Louisiana Separate Car Law.

Justice Brown's majority decision also claimed that the Louisiana state law did not conflict with the Thirteenth Amendment. In his argument, Tourgée had claimed that the Louisiana law had placed a "badge of servitude" on black passengers such as Plessy, thus placing the law in opposition to the Thirteenth Amendment. Brown managed to avoid Tourgée's claim, refusing to meet it in a straightforward, legal manner. He simply wrote that the Separate Car Law "does not conflict with the Thirteenth Amendment . . . is [a fact] too clear for argument."[93] In writing these words, Brown was choosing to narrowly interpret the Thirteenth Amendment's reference to prohibiting "slavery and involuntary servitude . . . a state of bondage; the ownership of mankind as chattel" as referring only specifically to legalized slavery. Justice Brown claimed that, because Louisiana was not holding Plessy

> Supreme Court of the United States,
>
> No. 210 , October Term, 1895.
>
> Homer Adolph Plessy
> Plaintiff in Error,
> vs.
> J. H. Ferguson, Judge of Section "A"
> Criminal District Court for the Parish
> of Orleans.
>
> In Error to the Supreme Court of the State of
> Louisiana
>
> This cause came on to be heard on the transcript of the
> record from the Supreme Court of the State of Louisiana,
> and was argued by counsel.
>
> On consideration whereof, It is now here ordered and
> adjudged by this Court that the judgment of the said Supreme
> Court, in this cause, be, and the same is hereby, affirmed
> with costs.
>
> Per Mr. Justice Brown,
> May 18, 1896.
> Dissenting:
> Mr. Justice Harlan

The verdict in the landmark Supreme Court case *Plessy v. Ferguson* reads, "It is now here ordered and adjudged by this Court that the judgment of the said Supreme Court, in this cause, be, and the same is hereby, affirmed."

in bondage as a slave, the state's car law and its requisite segregation did not amount to "a badge of servitude." Instead, the law implied "merely a legal distinction between the white and colored races."[94] Brown insisted that the Separate Car Law had not been created with the intention to "destroy the legal equality of the two races, or to reestablish a state of involuntary servitude."[95]

## THE SLAUGHTERHOUSE CASES

To bolster his interpretation of the legality of the Separate Car Law, Justice Brown cited earlier cases that served as precedents for *Plessy v. Ferguson*, including the Slaughterhouse Cases and the Civil Rights Cases. The Slaughterhouse Cases dated from a generation earlier, having been decided in 1873. The cases were the result of another Louisiana law, passed in 1869, that granted the sole privilege of slaughtering livestock in New Orleans to the Crescent City Live-Stock Landing and Slaughter-House Company. With the law constituting little more than a monopoly on the slaughtering business, butchers across the city protested and challenged it in court, claiming that it discriminated against them. Their lawyers used the Fourteenth Amendment to support their claim, arguing that the law was discriminatory because independent, non-company butchers could not do business in New Orleans.

In response to this legal challenge, the state of Louisiana claimed that the law had not been intended to discriminate, but rather to regulate the slaughtering industry. In the end, the U.S. Supreme Court agreed with the state and upheld the Louisiana statute. In making its decision, the Court explained that the equal protection clause of the Fourteenth Amendment applied only to state laws that discriminated against blacks as a class of citizens. This should have worked in favor of the Plessy supporters, but Brown and the court's majority had redefined the privileges and immunities of citizenship in the United States. Brown also used the Slaughterhouse Cases to deny that the Louisiana car law had violated the Thirteenth Amendment, stating, "It would be running the slavery argument into the ground to make it apply to every act of discrimination."[96]

Tourgée did not use the precedent of the Slaughterhouse Cases when making his case before the Louisiana Supreme Court because the decision in those cases was among the first of several used to reduce the right that blacks gained after the Civil War through the Fourteenth Amendment. He did, however, make reference to the cases in his brief to the United States Supreme Court. He did this to avoid it being used against him by his opposition. The Slaughterhouse Cases had established the precedent of weakening black rights. Tourgée had to cite other cases that seemed to contradict these damaging precedents. This allowed him to assert that "Plessy's exclusion from a first-class carriage was a deprivation of a basic right derived from his national, rather than his state, citizenship."[97] Working to his advantage was the fact that only one of the Supreme Court justices who had ruled on the Slaughterhouse Cases was still on the court: Justice Stephen J. Field had been one of the four justices who dissented from the majority opinion.

## THE CIVIL RIGHTS CASES

The Civil Rights Cases constituted another precedent for Brown's majority decision. These were a collection of five court cases that originated in five states: California, Kansas, Missouri, New York, and Tennessee. The cases were presented in 1883 in a single hearing simply because they spanned the same legal ground, namely the issue of race discrimination carried out by individuals against blacks. In two of the cases, blacks had been denied access to overnight accommodations; in two others, blacks had been banned from accessing a theater; and the fifth had a ring of the *Plessy* case about it, centering around a railroad's refusal to allow a black woman to board a passenger car set aside for white women. Samuel F. Phillips had served as the attorney for the five plaintiffs in the 1883 joint case. In filing the five cases, attorneys had claimed that each constituted a violation of the Civil Rights Act of 1875, which had banned discrimination on the grounds of race.

The Supreme Court had decided against the Civil Rights Cases, claiming that the Fourteenth Amendment intended to prevent only discrimination carried out by state governments, not that by individuals. The amendment did not grant Congress the power to ban discrimination by people but by institutions, companies, or businesses, including stores, theaters, places of amusement, hotels and inns, or transportation systems. Nevertheless, the 1883 Supreme Court decision had upheld the concept of "separate but equal" regarding accommodations on trains. As Brown used the Civil Rights Cases, he made the point that the Supreme Court had already made a practice of narrowly defining the Fourteenth Amendment.

## OTHER PRECEDENTS

Brown made use of other Supreme Court precedents in writing his majority decision. An 1876 decision, *U.S. v. Reese* had centered on the prosecution of two Kentucky election officials who had refused to count a vote cast by a black resident. Their actions, it was claimed, had violated the Fifteenth Amendment and the Civil Rights Act of 1870 (Enforcement Act). The Supreme Court had decided in favor of the election officials, however, claiming that Congress had gone beyond its powers by establishing the imposition of a heavy fine for denying someone the right to vote. The Court had decided that the "federal government had no powers other than those specifically mentioned by the Constitution and in neither that document nor the amendment was it given the power to assess penalties in local elections."[98] This 20-year-old decision provided a poor precedent for the advancement of the *Plessy* case against Louisiana.

Still another precedent used by Brown was the 1875 case *U.S. v. Cruikshank.* This case arose after an 1873 incident in Colfax Parish, Louisiana, during which a white mob had rioted and killed several hundred black people. Federal authorities indicted 16 of the white rioters under the Civil Rights Act of 1870 (Enforcement Act), which had banned actions that intended to "injure, oppress, threaten, or intimidate any citizen, with intent to prevent or hinder his free exercise and enjoyment of any right or privilege granted or secured to him by the constitution of laws of the United States."[99] The accused assailants were not convicted after the Supreme Court decided that the prosecution had not proven that the defendants had intended to specifically deny any rights to blacks. (In rendering this decision, the Court referred to the earlier precedent of the Slaughterhouse Cases.) Further, the Court ruled that the Fourteenth Amendment was designed only to secure "the individual from arbitrary exercise of the powers of the government." Because the actions against the black victims had been taken by white *individuals,* the Fourteenth Amendment did not apply. At the heart of this decision was the Court's claim that the case's prosecutors failed to show "that it was the intent of the defendants, by their conspiracy, to hinder or prevent the enjoyment of any right granted or secured by the Constitution."[100] In this same vein, Brown did not feel Plessy's lawyers had convinced the Court that the Separate Car Law denied blacks "the enjoyment of any right granted or secured by the Constitution."[101]

## HARLAN'S DISSENT

One lone justice dissented from the majority. He was Justice John Harlan. Most of the justices who upheld the constitutionality of the Separate Car Law were Northerners, but Harlan was from Kentucky, where, before the Civil War, he had been a slave owner.

In writing for the minority of one, Harlan assaulted the majority decision with a vengeance. He believed that the Separate Car Law was, in fact, a violation of the Thirteenth Amendment, interpreting the scope of the amendment to include more than simply the abolition of slavery. It "prevented the imposition of any burden or disabilities that constitute badges of slavery or servitude."[102] In his view of the car law, Harlan expressed his position that the law created such a "badge of servitude."

He cited in his decision that, in earlier decisions, the Supreme Court had established that America's railroads were public transportation systems, intended for use by everyone who could afford to buy a ticket, not just for a privileged class of people. The car law denied blacks and others of color an equal usage of these railroads. Someone such as Homer Plessy boarding a whites-only railcar was inevitable and reasonable in the face of the Separate Car Act, which, as Harlan wrote, regulated "the use of a public highway by citizens of the United States solely upon the basis of race."[103] Referring to Tourgée's presentation before the Court, Harlan reminded his colleagues of another obvious fact: "Every one knows," he wrote, that the Separate Car Law was created "not so much to exclude white persons from railroad cars occupied by blacks, as to exclude colored people from coaches . . . assigned to white persons."[104]

Harlan was even more adamant concerning the law's defiance of the Fourteenth Amendment. The majority decision seemed to consider the amendment something to struggle against by searching for loopholes, but Harlan considered it a glorious addition to the Constitution. He believed in the amendment's intention to guarantee the rights of all of America's citizens—not just one class. Relying on simple legal logic, Harlan stated the obvious concerning the two races and their access to public transportation, such as railroads: "If a white man and a black man choose to occupy the same public conveyance on a public highway, it is their right to do so and no government, proceeding alone on the grounds of race, can prevent it without infringing the personal liberty of each."[105]

It was this "liberty" that Harlan emphasized as he wrote regarding the attempt of one racial group to dominate another racial group. The law must not be held captive by those who hold power, whether economic, social, or political: "There is in this country no superior, dominant, ruling class of citizens. There is no caste here. Our Constitution is color-blind, and neither knows nor tolerates classes among citizens. In respect of civil rights, all citizens are equal before the law. The humblest is the peer of the most powerful."[106] Despite Harlan's sometimes eloquent dissent, the Supreme Court had decided and *Plessy v. Ferguson* would be upheld.

## THE END OF THE BATTLE

With the Supreme Court's decision, the Citizens' Committee's legal campaign came to an end. The committee had spent $2,700 in legal costs. With $166 left in its treasury, the committee gave $160 to local charities and the remaining $6 was used to pay for a testimonial for Albion Tourgée, who had campaigned on Plessy's behalf without pay. As for Homer Plessy, his life went on. He returned to New Orleans after the decision and took up his work as a shoemaker once more. (One of the first immediate results of the Supreme Court's decision for Plessy was that he

# JIM CROW LAW.

## UPHELD BY THE UNITED STATES SUPREME COURT.

### Statute Within the Competency of the Louisiana Legislature and Railroads—Must Furnish Separate Cars for Whites and Blacks.

Washington, May 18.—The Supreme Court today in an opinion read by Justice Brown, sustained the constitutionality of the law in Louisiana requiring the railroads of that State to provide separate cars for white and colored passengers. There was no interstate, commerce feature in the case for the railroad upon which the incident occurred giving rise to case—Plessey vs. Ferguson—East Louisiana railroad. was and is operated wholly within the State, to the laws of Congress of many of the States. The opinion states that by the analogy of the laws of Congress, and of many of states requiring establishment of separate schools for children of two races and other similar laws, the statute in question was within competency of Louisiana Legislature, exercising the police power of the State. The judgment of the Supreme Court of State upholding law was therefore upheld.

Mr. Justice Harlan announced a very vigorous dissent saying that he saw nothing but mischief in all such laws. In his view of the case, no power in the land had right to regulate the enjoyment of civil rights upon the basis of race. It would be just as reasonable and proper, he said, for states to pass laws requiring separate cars to be furnished for Catholic and Protestants, or for descendants of those of Teutonic race and those of Latin race,

A newspaper article announcing the *Plessy v. Ferguson* verdict notes that Justice Harlan's dissent argued that "no power in the land had right to regulate the enjoyment of civil rights upon the basis of race."

# THE AFTERMATH OF
## *PLESSY V. FERGUSON*

When the United States Supreme Court handed down the *Plessy v. Fer-guson* decision, it almost went without significant national notice. In the United States of 1896, few people cared whether the Court upheld yet another Jim Crow law. The day after the decision, the *New York Times* ran its story on page three of its second section, along with other run-of-the-mill railroad news. The *Times* did make reference to Justice Harlan's opinion, which was no surprise to the newspaper, since "he saw nothing but mischief in all such laws."* In New Orleans, the *Daily Picayune* lauded the Court's decision and, concerning the Separate Car Law, anxiously anticipated that "this regulation for the separation of the races will operate continuously on all lines of Southern railway."** In Richmond, Virginia, the *Dispatch* considered the value of the now-sanc-tioned Separate Car Law of Louisiana and wondered "whether such a law as that of Louisiana is not needed in all the Southern States."*** The reactions to the decision in Northern papers were less supportive, but they generally did not raise a major issue concerning the Court's ruling, either. The Springfield, Massachusetts, *Republican* did ask a mocking question regarding the decision's support of keeping the races sepa-rated: "Did the southerners ever pause to indict the Almighty for allow-ing Negroes to be born on the same earth with white men?"†

There would, indeed, be additional Jim Crow laws passed in the South in the years that followed. Eight southern states, Alabama, Flori-da, Georgia, Kentucky, Louisiana, Mississippi, Tennessee, and Texas, had created separate car laws before Plessy started his "test case" outside New Orleans in 1892. After the *Plessy* decision, others joined the pack: South Carolina in 1898, North Carolina the following year, Virginia in 1900, Maryland in 1904, and Oklahoma in 1907. Blacks soon came to be treated "virtually as lepers"†† by an increasingly powerful group of whites. New Jim Crow laws filled the statute books, segregating drinking fountains and public toilets and banning blacks from whites-only lunch counters and restaurants. All 11 Southern states from Maryland to Texas would continue to pass Jim Crow laws throughout the remainder of the 1890s and into the twentieth century, segregating not just railroad cars, but schools, libraries, parks, theaters, and public accommodations. There seemed to be no end to the expansion of segregation:

> [Blacks] had to use separate hospitals when they were ill, and, after they died, find their final rest in black cemeteries. Florida and North Carolina prohibited white children from using textbooks that had been touched by blacks. Alabama even made it a crime for blacks and whites to play checkers together. In Mississippi, blacks and whites had to use separate phone booths. Any Negro who inadvertently crossed the color line could expect to be severely punished.[†††]

Life would change for the nation's 8 million blacks after the *Plessy v. Ferguson* decision, and it would do so for the worse. In the aftermath, ripples of the decision would cause other millions of blacks yet unborn to struggle under the Supreme Court's establishment and legitimizing of "separate but equal" on a national scale. The concept would remain the law of the land for more than half a century.

---

*Quoted in Harvey Fireside, *Separate and Unequal: Homer Plessy and the Supreme Court Decision That Legalized Racism*. New York: Carroll & Graf Publishers, 2004, p. 223.

**Ibid.

***Ibid., p. 224.

†Ibid., p. 225.

††Ibid., p. 224.

†††Ibid.

John Marshall Harlan was the first Supreme Court justice to earn a modern law degree. Harlan served 34 years with the Court, one of the longest terms in history. He is regarded by many as one of the greatest visionaries the Supreme Court has ever seen.

had to appear in criminal court, again before Judge Ferguson, in January 1897, for violating the Separate Car Law. Ferguson offered him a choice of paying a $25 fine or going to jail. Plessy paid the fine.) For Plessy and the others who made up the city's Creole population, the future would turn differently. Where the Crescent City had been a largely tolerant community before the *Plessy* decision, it would turn on its black population, passing new Jim Crow laws that kept its colored citizens from attending public schools and using public accommodations. Plessy himself would live under the restraint of these laws for the remainder of this life, until his death in 1925. He was buried in the Catholic cemetery of St. Louis located along Basin Street. There was no special marker placed on his above-ground grave to note his defiant protest of Louisiana's Separate Car Law. His memory would live on, however, and his legacy would become the continuation of the struggle by others of his race to question, defy, challenge, and fight the racial prejudices bound to the pages of America's statute books, as well as those locked away in the human heart.

# Chronology

**1841** The state of Massachusetts adopts a law that requires separate rail passenger cars for blacks and whites, constituting the first known "Jim Crow" law.

**1857** With the *Dred Scott v. Sandford,* the United States Supreme Court decides that even free blacks do not have citizenship.

**1862** Homer Plessy is born a free black in the city of New Orleans.

**1863** President Abraham Lincoln issues the Emancipation Proclamation, freeing some of America's slave population.

**1865** The Thirteenth Amendment is ratified, bringing slavery in America to a legal end. That same month, white supremacist organization the Ku Klux Klan is established by former Confederates in Tennessee.

**1866** The 1866 Civil Rights Act guarantees certain rights to America's blacks and even implies that free blacks have American citizenship.

**1865–1868** Many former Confederate states in the South enact Black Codes.

**1867** The Reconstruction Act is passed by Congress.

**1868** The Fourteenth Amendment is ratified by the states, providing equal rights for blacks.

**1870** The last of the three Reconstruction Amendments, the Fifteenth, is ratified by the states, granting and guaranteeing blacks the right to vote.

**1871** Poll taxes are enacted by various Southern state legislatures as a means of disqualifying blacks from voting.

| 1873 | The U.S. Supreme Court decides the Slaughter-house Cases, choosing to restrict the interpretation of both the Thirteenth and Fourteenth Amendments. |
| 1875 | The Civil Rights Act is passed. |
| 1877 | The Reconstruction Era comes to an official end. |
| 1881 | Tennessee enacts the first discriminatory laws that include the wording "separate but equal." |
| 1883 | The U.S. Supreme Court decides on the unconstitutionality of the Civil Rights Act of 1875. |
| 1890 | The state of Louisiana passes its Separate Car Law. |
| 1891 | A group of New Orleans blacks organizes the Citizens' Committee with the intent to create a test case to challenge the constitutionality of Louisiana's Separate Car Law. |

# Timeline

**1841**
The state of Massachu-setts adopts the first known Jim Crow law.

**1866**
The 1866 Civil Rights Act guarantees certain rights to America's blacks.

**1875**
The Civil Rights Act is passed.

**1841**    third...... Congress shall make no law respecting a    **1881**

**December, 1865**
The Thirteenth Amendment is ratified.

**1868**
The Fourteenth Amendment is ratified.

**1870**
The last of the three Reconstruction Amendments, the Fifteenth, is ratified by the states.

**1881**
Tennessee passes one of the first "separate but equal" laws.

1891     The Citizens' Committee appoints Albion Tourgée as legal council.

1892     Daniel Desdunes boards a whites-only interstate railcar in an attempt to challenge the Separate Car Law in Louisiana.

1892     Homer Plessy boards an intrastate railcar to challenge Louisiana's Separate Car Law and is soon arrested.

1892     Judge John Ferguson decides on the Desdunes case, declaring Jim Crow laws regarding interstate travel unconstitutional.

1892     Judge Ferguson rules against Homer Plessy and upholds Louisiana's Separate Car Law. Plessy's lawyers soon file an appeal.

---

**1883**
The U.S. Supreme Court decides on the unconstitutionality of the Civil Rights At of 1875.

**September 1891**
The Citizens' Committee is organized.

**November 18, 1892**
Judge Ferguson rules against Homer Plessy.

**1883** — **1896**

**1890**
Louisiana passes its Separate Car Law.

**June 7, 1892**
Homer Plessy boards an "intrastate" railcar and is arrested.

**May 18, 1896**
The Supreme Court decides to uphold the constitutionality of Louisiana Separate Car Law."

1893     The Louisiana Supreme Court upholds the ruling of Judge Ferguson against Homer Plessy.

1895     Black leader Booker T. Washington delivers his Atlanta Exposition speech, which appears to sanction some forms of segregation between the races.

1896     The United States Supreme Court hears arguments regarding the *Plessy v. Ferguson* case.

1896     The Supreme Court decides to uphold the constitutionality of the Louisiana Separate Car Law.

1897     Plessy is charged the original fine of $25 for violating the Separate Car Laws in 1892.

# Notes

## Introduction

1. Quoted in Keith Weldon Medley, *We as Freemen: Plessy v. Ferguson* (Gretna, LA: Pelican Publishing Company, 2003, p. 142).
2. Quoted in Nathan Aaseng, *Plessy v. Ferguson: Separate but Equal* (San Diego: Lucent Books, 2003, p. 12).
3. Quoted in Harvey Fireside, *Separate and Unequal: Homer Plessy and the Supreme Court Decision That Legalized Racism* (New York: Carroll & Graf Publishers, 2004, p. 1).

## Chapter 1

4. Quoted in Darlene Clark Hine, *The African-American Odyssey* (Upper Saddle River, NJ: Prentice Hall, 2005, p. 277).
5. Ibid., pp. 295–296.
6. Ibid., p. 296.
7. Ibid., p. 263.
8. Ibid., p. 276.
9. Ibid., p. 285.
10. Ibid., p. 279.
11. Ibid., p. 298.

## Chapter 2

12. Quoted in Hine, *African-American Odyssey,* p. 310.
13. Ibid., p. 314.
14. Ibid., p. 315.
15. Quoted in Edward L. Ayers, *The Promise of the New South: Life After Reconstruction* (New York: Oxford University Press, Inc., 1992, p. 136).
16. Ibid., p. 132.
17. Ibid., p. 136.
18. Ibid.
19. Ibid., p. 316.
20. Ibid., p. 136.
21. Ibid., p. 137.
22. Ibid.

## Chapter 3

23. Quoted in C. Vann Woodward, *The Strange Career of Jim Crow* (New York: Oxford University Press, 1957, p. xiii).
24. Ibid., p. 70.
25. Ibid., p. 18
26. Quoted in Aaseng, *Plessy v. Ferguson,* p. 36.

27. Quoted in William H. Chafe, et al., eds., *Remembering Jim Crow: African-Americans Tell About Life in the Segregated South* (New York: New Press, 2001, p. 72).
28. Quoted in Charles A. Lofgren, *The Plessy Case:A Legal-Historical Interpretation* (New York: Oxford University Press, 1987, p. 12).
29. Quoted in Fireside, *Strange Career,* p. 98.
30. Quoted in Aaseng, *Plessy v. Ferguson,* p. 43.
31. Quoted in Medley, *We as Freemen,* p. 81.

**Chapter 4**
32. Quoted in Medley, *We as Freemen,* p. 83.
33. Ibid., p. 85.
34. Ibid., p. 92.
35. Ibid., p. 91.
36. Quoted in Ayers, *Promise of the New South,* p. 139.
37. Ibid.
38. Quoted in Medley, *We as Freemen,* p. 92.
39. Ibid., p. 93.
40. Ibid., p. 94.
41. Ibid., p. 95.
42. Ibid., p. 97.
43. Ibid., p. 98.
44. Quoted in Aaseng, *Plessy v. Ferguson,* p. 44.
45. Quoted in Medley, *We as Freemen,* pp. 108–109.
46. Ibid., p. 109.

**Chapter 5**
47. Ibid., p. 113.
48. Quoted in Aaseng, *Plessy v. Ferguson,* p. 47.
49. Ibid., p. 49.
50. Ibid., p. 50.
51. Ibid.
52. Quoted in Medley, *We as Freemen,* pp. 156–157.
53. Ibid., p. 157.

**Chapter 6**
54. Ibid., p. 22.
55. Ibid., p. 25.
56. Ibid., p. 26.
57. Ibid., p. 32.
58. Ibid., p. 34.
59. Ibid., p. 39.
60. Quoted in Albert J. Von Frank, *The Trials of Anthony Burns* (Cambridge, MA: Harvard University Press, 1977, p. 130).

**Chapter 7**
61. Quoted in Joan B. Garvey and Mary Lou Widmer, *Beautiful Crescent: A History of New Orleans.* New Orleans: Garmer Press, 1982, p. 155.
62. Quoted in "The Order of Knights of Pythias," www.pythias.org/pythstory/
63. Quoted in Medley, *We as Freedmen,* p. 161.
64. Ibid., p. 162.
65. Ibid.
66. Quoted in Fireside, *Separate and Unequal,* p. 116.

67. Quoted in Brook Thomas, *Plessy v. Ferguson: A Brief History with Documents.* Boston: Bedford Books, 1997, p. 12.
68. Quoted in Fireside, *Separate and Unequal,* p. 119.
69. Ibid., p. 120.
70. Ibid., p. 121.
71. Ibid., p. 122.
72. Ibid., p. 123.
73. Ibid.

**Chapter 8**

74. Quoted in Keith Weldon Medley, "For Homer Plessy, 'separate' was not 'equal'" (*Smithsonian Magazine* 24 February 1994, 11:104).
75. Ibid., p. 114.
76. Quoted in Aaseng, *Plessy v. Ferguson,* p. 54.
77. Ibid.
78. Quoted in Medley, *We as Freedmen,* p. 193.
79. Quoted in Medley, "For Homer Plessy," p. 115.
80. Quoted in Medley, *We as Freedmen,* p. 177.
81. Ibid., p. 199.
82. Ibid., p. 201.
83. Ibid.
84. Ibid.

85. Ibid.
86. Ibid.
87. Quoted in Fireside, *Separate and Unequal,* p. 195.
88. Quoted in Medley, *We as Freedmen,* p. 201.
89. Quoted in Aaseng, *Plessy v. Ferguson,* p. 60.
90. Ibid.
91. Quoted in Thomas, *Plessy v. Ferguson,* p. 30.
92. Ibid.

**Chapter 9**

93. Quoted in Fireside, *Separate and Unequal,* p. 203.
94. Ibid.
95. Ibid.
96. Ibid.
97. Ibid., p. 130.
98. Quoted in Aaseng, *Plessy v. Ferguson,* p. 66.
99. Ibid., p. 65.
100. Ibid.
101. Ibid.
102. Ibid., p. 76.
103. Quoted in Fireside, *Separate and Unequal,* p. 216.
104. Ibid.
105. Quoted in Aaseng, *Plessy v. Ferguson,* p. 77.
106. Quoted in Fireside, *Separate and Unequal,* p. 217.

# Glossary

**Abolitionist**  A person who worked to bring an end to slavery.

**amendment**  A change to a piece of legislation.

**dissent**  The non-majority opinion in a Supreme Court case.

**docket**  A record of proceedings in a legal action.

**infraction**  A violation.

**integrate**  To incorporate people from different groups.

**Ku Klux Klan**  A twentieth century secret society advocating white supremacy.

**Jim Crow law**  Legal enforcement of discrimination against blacks.

**martial law**  Temporary rule of a civilian population by military authorities during a time of emergency.

**mulatto**  A person with black and white ancestry.

**segregation**  The separation of a race or group from others.

**statute**  An act or law that is created through legislation.

**suffrage**  The right to vote.

**Reconstruction**  The period after the U.S. Civil War when the Southern states were integrated back into the Union.

# Bibliography

Aaseng, Nathan. *Plessy v. Ferguson: Separate but Equal.* San Diego, Calif.: Lucent Books, 2003.

Ayers, Edward L. *The Promise of the New South: Life After Reconstruction.* New York: Oxford University Press, 1992.

Chafe, William H., et al., eds., *Remembering Jim Crow: African-Americans Tell About Life in the Segregated South.* New York: New Press, 2001.

Davis, Ronald L.F. "Creating Jim Crow: In-Depth Essay." Available online. url:http://www.jimcrowhistory.org/history/creating2.htm.

Fireside, Harvey. *Separate and Unequal: Homer Plessy and the Supreme Court Decision That Legalized Racism.* New York: Carroll & Graf Publishers, 2004.

Garvey, Joan B., and Mary Lou Widmer. *Beautiful Crescent: A History of New Orleans.* New Orleans: Garmer Press, 1982.

Hine, Darlene Clark. *The African-American Odyssey.* Upper Saddle River, NJ: Prentice Hall, 2005.

Lofgren, Charles A. *The Plessy Case: A Legal-Historical Interpretation.* New York: Oxford University Press, 1987.

Medley, Keith Weldon. "For Homer Plessy, 'separate' was not 'equal.'" *Smithsonian Magazine* 24 11; February 1994 :104.

———. *We as Freemen: Plessy v. Ferguson.* Gretna, La.: Pelican Publishing Company, 2003.

Thomas, Brook. *Plessy v. Ferguson: A Brief History with Documents.* Boston: Bedford Books, 1997.

Von Frank, Albert J. *The Trials of Anthony Burns.* Cambridge, Mass.: Harvard University Press, 1977.

Woodward, C. Vann. *The Strange Career of Jim Crow.* New York: Oxford University Press, 1957.

# Further Reading

Anderson, Wayne. *Plessy v. Ferguson: Legalizing Segregation.*
New York: Rosen Publishing Group, 2003.

Marcus, Robert D. *American Firsthand, Segregation and Plessy and Brown.* Boston: Bedford/St. Martin's, 2002.

Olsen, Otto. *Thin Disguise: Turning Point in Negro History: Plessy vs. Ferguson, a Documentary Presentation, 1864–1896.* New York: Brill Academic Publishers, Inc., 1967.

Roark, James L. *American Promise: Plessy vs. Ferguson.* Boston: Bedford/St. Martin's, 2002.

**Web Sites**

www.afroamhistory.about.com/library/blplessy_v_ferguson.htm
www.landmarkcases.org/plessy/background3.html
www.law.umkc.edu/faculty/projects/ftrials/conlaw/plessy.html
www.oyez.org/oyez/resource/case/307/
www.usinfo.state.gov/usa/infousa/facts/democrac/33.htm
www.watson.org/~lisa/blackhistory/post-civilwar/plessy.html

# Picture Credits

10: The Historic New Orleans Collection, accession no. 1974.25.37.57

14: Getty Images

15: National Archives and Records Administration

19: The New York Public Library/ Art Resource, NY

23: National Archives and Records Administration

27: Library of Congress Prints and Photographs Division

30: Library of Congress Prints and Photographs Division

35: ©CORBIS

37: The Granger Collection, New York

41: Library of Congress Prints and Photographs Division

44: Library of Congress Prints and Photographs Division

48: ©Hulton-Deutsch Collection/ CORBIS

50: Print Collection, Miriam and Ira D. Wallach Division of Art, Prints and Photographs, The New York Public Library, Astor, Lenox and Tilden Foundations

53: Library of Congress Prints and Photographs Division

59: General Research & Reference Division, Schomburg Center for Research in Black Culture, The New York Public Library, Astor, Lenox and Tilden Foundations

66: Chautauqua County Historical Society, Westfield, NY

69: ©CORBIS

76: The Granger Collection, New York

80: The Granger Collection, New York

82: Getty Images

87: Robert N. Dennis Collection of Stereoscopic Views, Miriam & Ira D. Wallach Division of Art, Prints & Photographs, The New York Public Library, Astor, Lenox and Tilden Foundations

91: Supreme Court of Louisiana Historical Archives, Earl K. Long Library, University of New Orleans.

96: The Historic New Orleans Collection, accession no. 1974.25.37.10

102: Library of Congress Prints and Photographs Division

106: Library of Congress Prints and Photographs Division

111: National Records and Archives Administration

117: The Granger Collection, New York

120: Library of Congress Prints and Photographs Division

Cover: Library of Congress Prints and Photographs Division

# Index

# About the Author

Tim McNeese is an associate professor of history at York College, in York, Nebraska, where he is in his fifteenth year of college instruction. Professor McNeese earned his associate of arts degree from York College, a bachelor of arts in history and political science from Harding University, and a master of arts in history from Southwest Missouri State University. A prolific author of books for elementary, middle, high school, and college readers, McNeese has published more than 75 books and educational materials over the past 20 years on everything from Mississippi steamboats to Marco Polo. His writing has earned him a citation in the library reference work, *Something About the Author*. In 2005, he published the textbook *Political Revolutions of the 18th, 19th, and 20th Centuries*. Professor McNeese served as a consulting historian for the History Channel program, "Risk Takers, History Makers." His wife, Beverly, is an assistant professor of English at York College, and they have two children, Noah and Summer. Readers are encouraged to contact Professor McNeese at tdmcneese@york.edu.